First published in Great Britain in 1997 by
POETRY NOW
1-2 Wainman Road, Woodston,
Peterborough, PE2 7BU
Telephone (01733) 230746
Fax (01733) 230751

All Rights Reserved

Copyright Contributors 1997

HB ISBN 1 86188 705 1
SB ISBN 1 86188 700 0

FOREWORD

Although we are a nation of poetry writers we are accused of not reading poetry and not buying poetry books: after many years of listening to the incessant gripes of poetry publishers, I can only assume that the books they publish, in general, are books that most people do not want to read.
Poetry should not be obscure, introverted, and as cryptic as a crossword puzzle: it is the poet's duty to reach out and embrace the world.
The world owes the poet nothing and we should not be expected to dig and delve into a rambling discourse searching for some inner meaning.
The reason we write poetry (and almost all of us do) is because we want to communicate: an ideal; an idea; or a specific feeling. Poetry is as essential in communication, as a letter; a radio; a telephone, and the main criteria for selecting the poems in this anthology is very simple: they communicate.
'Beneath the rule of men entirely great, the pen is mightier than the sword' E G Bulaver-Lytton
The subject of war has been an issue which has inspired poets for many years and it is still a popular subject for today's poets.
Killing Fields - When Enough is Enough is a modern collection of poetry all about war. The poems inside look at all aspects of war in a realistic way. Some of the poems are emotive, some opinionated and some just simply bring home the evil of war.
Whilst some may claim that writing about war is morbid, the majority will agree that through poetry we can reflect on the issues of war and show everyone how unnecessary and horrifying war is.

CONTENTS

What's The Point?	Violette Edwards	1
Guns and Tears	June Davies	2
War Requiem	Suzette Childeroy Compton	2
Too Late?	Sylvia Dargue	3
The Hero	Lucy Crisp	3
A British Soldier	Margaret C Rae	4
Our World	Shahnaz Choudhury	6
For King And Country	M Clark	6
Why?	Victoria L Williams	7
War	C Gaunt	8
Bombs Away!	Julian Collins	8
A Gateway to Perfidy	A R Price	9
Artillery Man	Richard Fraser	10
Long Night Of Doom	Ron Matthews Jr	11
On Joining The WAAF	Dorothy Mezaks	12
A Soldier's Prayer	J S Liberkowski	13
Phantom	Stuart Winfield	14
Perpetual Light	Lorna May	14
Heroes	L Rye	15
The Death Of Hope	Radovan Visnjic	16
With Lines Drawn	S Sutton	17
The Least	M R Mackinnon-Pattison	18
Some Mother's Son	Thomas Boyle	19
V E Day	M J Stirling	20
Together For Victory	Vera Graver	21
The Vision	Russell Humphrey	22
Another War	L Barnett	23
Mind The Doors Please	Marion Lawson	24
Silent Tears	Frances McHugh	24
Monte Cassino	Bernard Johnston	25
The Blameless Moderate	Ann McAreavey	26
War Memorial	Diana Momber	27
Trieste - 1945	John W Dossett-Davies	28
A Klic Too Far	Terry Bates	29
Blood Storm	Stephen Gyles	30
Sixteen	Alan Charles	31

I Don't Want To Be Here	Jenny Chamberlain	32
The Toymakers	Eric Allday	33
Fly By Nights?	Deane Wynne	34
He Died A Hero	J Stanbury	35
As Was And Is	Henry J Green	36
Just One Word, War!	S M Bush-Payne	37
We Take Life For Granted	Eda Singleton	38
Not Forgotten	Frances Gibson	39
A Point Of View	R Garrett	40
Fertile Fields	Tamar Segal	41
Cologne	Peter Marshall	42
The Prisoner Of War	Bert Richings	43
Thoughts Of War	Mike Coyle	44
Old And Young	Fred Brown	44
Not On My Street	Mary Brackley	45
The Killing Fields	C O Desjarlais	46
Diary Of War	Eileen Boden	47
Society Doesn't Care	Ann Willbourne	48
Who Will Tell?	B Tully	48
A Survivor Of War	H Fox	49
The Night London Was Ablaze	L J Culbert	50
Don't Stop Trying	Deborah Butcher	51
War Time	Liam St Clair	52
Peace Or War?	W L Oakley	52
The Poppies Remembered ...	Gemma Titchener	53
Death Wish	Angela Lansbury	54
Wars Fade	Alan Jones	55
Some Mother's Son	Joy Nethercot	56
Balkan Rhapsody	Charlie Maunsell	57
Peace	Hilary Mason	58
A Brief History Of War	Daniel R Deakin	59
The Evacuee	J Newman	60
Green Fields	Iris Kelly	61
Letter	S Hine	62
Cross-Fire Or The Cross	R Peter Smith	63
Far Beyond A World A Man Weeps	Claudia	64
Africa Again	Joy Aldridge	64

Little White Crosses	Polly Bennison	65
A Killing Field	D W Owen	66
When War Will Be No More	M A Atkinson	66
Casualties Of War	J E Simpkins	67
The Soldier	I Vincent	68
Cold	Charles Thomson	69
The Message	Barbara Froggatt	70
The Banquet	B J Jones	70
Evacuated	M Hume	71
Every One A Mother's Son	T D Watson	72
Stop Think	Kathleen Scarborough	73
Belfast . . .	Bernadette Kennedy	74
Flags And Tears	M T Breslin	74
Borderline	M Mickley	75
Tommy	David Brownley	76
It Wasn't Me	Richard Ball	77
Last Christmas	Ronald Parr	78
Our Friends Lie There	Brian Gregan	80
Too Young To Die	E K Wood	80
Why Have Wars!	Josephine Quinn	81
Blood Harvest	Stephen Gyles	82
Silent Numbers	Cathrine Campbell Rogers	83
The Attack	Reg Curwen	84
Swords And Shares	Paul Thompson	85
War	K Stackhouse	86
War Child	Jennifer Statham	86
Soldiers	Judith E Lowe	87
No Surrender	C Brady	88
Killing Time	Kathy Squires	89
Prisoners Of Time	Mary Joyce Baxter	90
Peace Is Finished	Albert Wilson	91
Monsters	J Smith	92
Strangers	Jane Bhadal	93
A Soldier's Tale	Gina Charles	94
Don't Weep For Me (Yugoslavia)	D W Owen	95
Bad Memories	Beryl Spanswick	96
Then And Now	Beatrice Jones	96

Compassion	Ruth Kirkham	97
Brothers	José Herron	98
War Games, 1914-1918	Colin Dudley	99
Sea Of Poppies	D Selbie	100
Sabotage	James Stevenson	100
Tears Roll Down	Greg King	101
In This Age	Ann Hubbard	102
Armageddon	Julia Eva Yeardye	103
What It Would Be Like	Steven Hunter	104
View From Death Hill	Arda Lacey	104
The Uninvited Guest	Teresa Whaley	105
Forgiven	Phil Simpson	106
What Price A Life	S Griffiths	107
Dead Soldier Reincarnation	David Miller	108
The Theatre Of War	G Kenny	109
Lord Havoc!	C N Messenger	110
The Darkest Moments	Kevin Murphy	110
Living To Fight	Zenda Cooper	111
Stop, You're Killing Me	T Pemberton	112
Brave Soldier	Peter Frost	112
Prisoners Of War	Lauren Sirey	113
War Again	J Dunkley	114
Bert 1641095	E Merritt	115
Remembrance	Dennis Brockelbank	116
Our Garden In Winter	J Nolan	117
Where Lies	Mark Andrew Phillips	118
Summer Of 1940	Anthony Clarke	119
Battle Cry	P K Church	120
The Holocaust	J W Hayes	121
Someone To Blame	Philip Q Mills	122
At War!	B M Lennox	123
The Silence	Clarissa Fear	123
The Waugh Against Crime	James Stevenson	124

WHAT'S THE POINT?

Tufts of grass try to grow midst the rubble.
Sunlight barely enhances the scene.
A young woman's tears fall freely.
She recalls the field once grassy green.

Desolate now, almost forbidding.
Long gone its original charm.
Her gait unsteady, hardly surprising.
With one leg left; just one good arm.

Memory for her became crystal clear.
Shivers crept down her spine.
Luckier than her two younger brothers.
Holding hands when they stepped on a mine.

What possible need had there been for Gas Chambers?
How could they count the cost?
Refugees disappearing from the face of the earth.
Someone knew all too well, they'd be lost.

What point to destroy homes? The families?
Be it tent, mansion or shack.
Because maybe their beliefs were different?
Tormentors never think back.

It's a figure of speech, 'war to end all wars'.
Use your tongues. Time to lower all shields.
To bathe in Earth's wonders, to walk without fear.
On a grassy path; not Killing Fields.

Violette Edwards

GUNS AND TEARS

I am just a simple soldier
A servant of the Queen
Yet tears and grief invade my heart
For the horrors that I've seen
You may think I'm insensitive
And things don't go too deep
But with all the pictures in my mind
I find it hard to sleep
I've seen my comrades blown apart
I've heard their cries of pain
And through the guns and blood and smoke
You wonder if you're sane
For all wars are a tragedy
There is no gain or plus
But when it comes to evil
It's sometimes them or us
So we must guard the innocent
Do our duty, to right wrong
May God forgive our human faults
And help to make us strong.

June Davies

WAR REQUIEM

Death greets Life
With a spectral smile:
Life greets Death
With insufficient guile
And the one asks the other
If it's all worthwhile.

Suzette Childeroy Compton

TOO LATE?

Can we learn, or is it too late
That it's as easy to love, as it is to hate
The earth grows weary of continual strife
As people, animals and plants fight for life
We've taken for granted the fruits of the earth
Now for many there's no chance of re-birth
There was enough for everyone's need
Not enough for everyone's greed
War and pollution what chance have we got
Half the world starves while food mountains rot
A barren world is our children's tomorrow
A world of fear, of famine and sorrow

Sylvia Dargue (deceased)

THE HERO

'Come back a hero!'
Urged his mother,
Waving goodbye
With a spotted handkerchief.
He came back,
Mindless,
His beautiful face distorted by
Scars.
He begged in the streets,
Playing a mouth-organ
Tunelessly.
His mother,
Dressed in black,
Passed him by
Not knowing who he
Was!

Lucy Crisp

A British Soldier

I fought for my country
In the Crimean War
I was glad to go
They couldn't ask for more
I fought for my country
I was in the Light Brigade
I took part in the charge
And died where I laid

I fought for my country
In World War One
They said they needed me
They gave me a gun
I fought for my country
In the trenches I died
I was there at the Somme
It was my mother who cried

I fought for my country
In World War Two
I flew in an aeroplane
Right up in the blue
I fought for my country
I flew and I died
In the Battle of Britain
It was my wife who cried

I fought for my country
In the Korean War
I volunteered to go
I didn't ask what for
I fought for my country
In a foreign land I died
I didn't know the reason
It was my sweetheart who cried

I fought for my country
In the Falklands this time
I served on a ship
In this alien clime
I fought for my country
In our ship I died
There was no time for escape
This time no one cried

I fought for my country
Now Hussein was our foe
In tanks painted pink
With sand the only view
I fought for my country
Amid burning sands
They said it was friendly fire
We died at our allies' hands

I fought for my country
In every war there was
I fought hard in them all
I supported every cause
I fought for my country
A British soldier to the core
I fought for the government
But I'll fight no more.

Margaret C Rae

Our World

An unshed single tear
to quench the thirst of a child.
Cries of a little one heard.
The remains of a meal
to satisfy a famished village,
Is this our world?

Innocent eyes of a little girl
witnessing violence, rage and death.
A victim's father, heartless to forgive.
The loss of a mother, a stolen breath.
A new-born baby lives.

We are part of the human race
but the prejudice we still face,
thrives on our fear.
It was no better yesterday
but no longer should we hide away.

      The white dove, a free bird.
      Peace and love, this should be our world.

Shahnaz Choudhury

For King And Country

Through the haze of cordite,
From painful half-closed eyes.
A single tear rolls down his cheek,
As he watches his best friend die.

His heart is filled with anguish,
For every mother's son,
Who leaves his home so full of pride,
To die by an unknown gun.

His sorrow slowly turns to hate,
But who does he really despise?
Those who fire the bullets?
Or those in collars and ties?

M Clark

WHY?

'Daddy won't be coming home,
He's gone to live with God,
To be an angel in Paradise,'
The child could only nod.

But why won't he return to us?
Why has he gone to live up there?
What about the things we haven't done?
The times we were supposed to share?

And everyone says I must be brave,
And look after Mummy now.
But that was always Daddy's job,
And I just don't know how.

How to make her laugh like Daddy did,
When she sits and stares into space.
How to make everything alright again,
To stop the tears drying on her face.

And no-one else can understand,
They mumble about it being sad,
As the flag-draped coffin passes by,
On top lies the beret of my Dad.

Victoria L Williams

WAR

In a cloud of dust the tanks and guns go by,
Gaunt shells of buildings stand etched against the sky,
This once was home,
Here they slept, ate, laughed and wept
And had their being.
No, don't pass on friend, stop!
Look at man's inhumanity.

Wizened faces old all beyond their years,
Black with dirt and streaked with tears,
Thin bodies, bellies swollen with hunger
And sores and neglect.
Hopeless and helpless, the backwash of war
Sitting in the gutter.
You can't help? Stop and think again.

When you were young you came to no harm,
You were loved and cared for, fed and warm.
Each and all suffer in wars
Everyone bears the scars.
You have been young, you have yet to be old.
Pause now my friend, accept the load.

C Gaunt

BOMBS AWAY!

and that the day the bombs came down
I drove my chauffeur into town
and wondered how the bird had flown
within a world of upside down

I heard the sirens, saw the planes,
smelt the tongues of angry flames,
counted out insurance claims
and felt my collar buried under
piles of debris, homes made empty,
rows of fat and frantic lanes
of spent and squandered Christian names.

Julian Collins

A GATEWAY TO PERFIDY

Dark clouds formed in an ominous clutch
perpetrating a peace-loving sky, it was
midnight or hours quite near suddenly
long knives of yellow pierced the darkness
and we knew that people would die.

Oh war, the splintering of glass,
the crashing of bricks the cries of dying
souls who harmed no one, the war could
not be won by us with devious tricks.

I as an innocent child, stood
watching, close to tears after the siren
wailed I still stood watching, then it
appeared, we called it the Buzz Bomb
lethargic accuracy with that faint buzz
of so near silence, it sped to its
target. no pilot what a plot, it came to
a halt up there in the sky, then
plummeted to kill more people another
peace-loving home destroyed, and more
would die.

A R Price

Artillery Man

A town is burning
in a far off land,
a broken doll lies by a severed hand,
a painful end
to a short lifespan,
one more kill for the artillery man.

You adjust your aim
and the barrel climbs higher,
there are a thousand lives
in your line of fire,
you wait and listen
as they breathe their last,
falling to the force of the concussion blast.
As the shrapnel rips
you hear their screams,
your dreams are their nightmares,
your nightmares their dreams.

Amidst the twisted broken limbs
the wheels of a skateboard
slowly spin.
Legs lie close by,
no shoes, no feet,
a lifeless face stares up from the street.
A small boy dies
in a stranger's arms,
one more kill for the artillery man.

Richard Fraser

LONG NIGHT OF DOOM

I do not know; I was not there;
I cannot say; I know not where;
The tears; The bloodshed; The pain; The futility;
I missed them all, you ask, do *I* care?

Beaches soaked with blood of many;
Ruined cities in piles there, of rubble . . .
. . . rotting corpses littering killing fields,
Limed remains - beginning or end, of trouble?

Do not cast your aspersion upon me,
for only young am I and witness not;
The scale of wars tho' unlikened,
I was not there; not one of those, sadly, shot . . .

. . . and tho' the walls of honour fell
into pots of depths bathed in evil gloom
and despots rule began to wane,
the world did witness, that long night of saturated doom.

'Here endeth the lesson' or so we hoped,
An end to bloodletting and weeping wives and others who care . . .
. . . an end to war and strife and death,
not that I believe such empty words and promises,
                frenzied out of fear;
                of death;
                of prolonged pain of life

mayhap such dictation uttered? I cannot say,

            I was not there . . .

Ron Matthews Jr

ON JOINING THE WAAF

I decided one day I must go to war
To keep those Gerrys from our shore.
So up I got on a cold winter's morn.
It was rough and raw at the crack of dawn.

At last I was ready and raring to go.
I opened the back door, it was waist-high in snow.
My Dad was there to clear me a path.
My mother cried, but I had to laugh.
It was that, or I would break down in tears
If I did that, it would haunt me for years.

So off I set, to catch the train.
I didn't know when I'd see Shirebrook again
I met more recruits on the way there.
We were all the same with fears to share.
Off to Bridgnorth, the coldest place on earth.
We will soon be able to show our worth.

At last the RAF transport came.
Soon we would all be dressed the same.
First the sergeant we'd be meeting.
I hope we get a very nice greeting.
We were all feeling very much in awe!
We'd heard about these sergeants before.
But we really had no reason to fret.
After all, we'd done nothing wrong *not yet.*

The sergeant told us a thing or two
About what to do, and what not to do.
One thing I couldn't get out of my head.
She said, 'You'll find three biscuits on your bed.'
So tired and hungry we all did feel.
I thought well, that isn't much of a meal.
The biscuits were three mattresses in a heap
On which we were intended to sleep.
When I realised that, I did feel green.
But things like that, I'd never seen.

We went for a proper meal in due course.
We were so hungry, we could have eaten a horse.
The shepherd's pie how good it tasted.
There wasn't one little scrap got wasted.
We got all our kit the very next day.
Then we were posted to Morecambe Bay.
What with marching, PT and loads of drill
By the end of five weeks; we'd had our fill.
Our feet were blistered and extremely sore.
But in *spite of all this, we must* win this war
With the drilling ended, we were soon to be parted.
We couldn't help feeling a bit downhearted.
But we had various jobs for which we had to train
And who knows, we could meet up again.

Dorothy Mezaks

A SOLDIER'S PRAYER

Who sanctions this action,
Therefore who absolves my soul?
Hold your breath . . .
                Squeeze the trigger tightly.
Who is this shape,
That I now sight before me?
Hold your breath . . .
                Squeeze the trigger tightly.

Sharp . . . is the crack,
As they fall like a broken puppet,
Release the trigger . . .
                Breathe out quickly.
But who sanctions my action,
And who will absolve my soul.

J S Liberkowski

PHANTOM

A row of medals,
keen as jewelled suns,
scatter time as refracted light.

He owns no uniform,
loses unity,
lies naked,
alone,
in a room where only the dead breathe.

Photograph of a smiling woman,
alongside a bloodstained wallet,
a horrible form lives inside
a dumbfounded heart.

'Forever,' the lovers declare,
there is no limit to our faith.

Words float in a lucid sky,
above and beyond the call
of earthbound duty.

Stuart Winfield

PERPETUAL LIGHT

Believe it happened then my friend
and still today the inhumane acts
of time leap into lives innocent
chaste, illumined in splendour

Darkest deeds of ignorance and hate
monopolise the media subtracting
from focus the task of love and care
predestined for our human race

Weep my friend for cruel acts of
injustice are born still though
not without judgement do those
perpetrators sink in sands of time

Look beyond indignities of our world
keep your integrity intact with truth
and beauty to shine through your
soul penetrating time and eternity

Lorna May

HEROES

They're all heroes to me.
Those brave brave men.
Men they were too, even the boys.
To go over the hill
Into what they didn't know, screaming out loud.
        With their bayonets all aglow
Running and screaming, screaming and running
With just one direction to go
All straight ahead men, faster they ran.
Through the mist and the gunsmoke,
Most didn't run they just fell
But the rest kept on running over that hill.
Running for me, you.
Every free person in the world.

L Rye

THE DEATH OF HOPE

I had lain on the ground for so long
that I cannot remember how I got
here, or how I came to bleed,
and then I saw that I was among
other people who had got badly shot,
and I was in pain and in need,

The people around me were in pain,
screaming with half their bellies out
upon the dirt and the blood rushing
out of the wounds awashed with the rain,
which fell from the skies, and I shout,
kicking and shaking and then pushing.

But nothing makes any more difference,
in this war of mutual anger, this hatred
denies me my right as a human being
to be treated fairly and with reverence,
and some ugly moron has just berated
me for crying and for my pleading.

That last kick in my stomach hurt me,
a leather boot into the gut, my eyes bulge
ready to pop out of my sockets and I feel
sick and then pass out and collapse
into a world in which I cannot indulge.

There was no awakening, coming to life
and that last act of violence killed me,
releasing my soul from the horrible tortures.
I left behind two little boys and my wife
who now stand at my graveside and weep,
unable to predict each of their sad futures.

Radovan Visnjic

WITH LINES DRAWN

Napalm, land-mines, carpet-bombing
Machine-guns, flame-throwers, gas,
Hand-grenades, missiles, short range mortars;
Technology gone mad, alas.

Gainsborugh, Constable, Leonardo Da Vinci,
Copernicus unravelling space;
Gallileo, Pythagorus, Darwin and Einstein,
Can this be the same human race?

Mussolini, Hitler, Amin, Pol-Pot;
Viet-Cong and Nazi inducing fear of the name.
Mother Theresa, Alfred Nobel, Dr Barnado,
These are the two sides of the same.

Mass graves, executions, genocide, rape;
Some humans are proud they took part,
Marie Curie, Florence Nightingale, Luther King, Jesus Christ;
Whilst these humans all gave from the heart.

We all sometimes go a bit over the top,
A gesture, an insult, we all do it,
As individuals we all recover from this
But as mankind, can we get though it?

Down through the ages come Attila The Hun,
Vlad The Impaler, and everyone;
Diogenese, Socrates and Plato give battle:

Warfare. Is it sounding our species death-rattle?

S Sutton

THE LEAST

The hand stretched into nowhere,
   Clasped nothing and faded away;
Life that was born - tomorrow's child
   Expired at the end of the day.
It died from malnutrition,
   Disease, or crushed by machine:
Doubt cried 'Rights and Freedom,'
   The child was caught between.

The voice that asked for reason
   Received a silent reply;
The child that greeted the morning
   By night would unreasoned die.
Its unheard cry for mercy,
   The helpless facing its doom:
A whisper in the corner of
   A distant sound-proof room.

The eyes that sought for beauty
   Gazed lost on a desert waste;
A mouth that craved for sweetness,
   Found bitter in the taste.
Tears from patience weakening,
   How long can patience wait?
Maybe tomorrow; tomorrow - but
   Tomorrow must be too late.

The ears that strained for laughter
   Heard naught but the insect's flight:
Shall you - shall you, tomorrow's child,
   Inherit freedom and right?
Our blindness - your freedom to suffer,
   Our deafness - your freedom to cry;
Our disconcern we give today
   Your only right - to die.

M R Mackinnon-Pattison

SOME MOTHER'S SON

He was his parents' pride and joy,
A dare-devil teenage soldier boy.
With laughing eyes and beardless chin,
He captivated with his boyish grin.

His mother shed many a bitter tear,
As she watched him buckle his bandolier.
Before marching away to fight the foe,
Other young men he did not know.

Soon he found himself in a trench,
With bloodied mud and sewer-like stench.
Listening to comrades cry for their mother,
Before the poison gas their cries did smother.

In the opposite trench a youth's fair head,
A pull on the trigger and he was dead.
Well away from the front, in some chateau,
Generals were drinking wine, and eating gateau.

Then one day the war, it was all over,
And our young hero returned to Dover.
He looked much older than his years,
And he had no eyes, to shed his tears.

His mother, who fed him from her breast,
Wished her blind son, wasn't so depressed.
Sometimes she thought, the fruit of her womb,
Wouldn't be happy this side of the tomb.

Up and down the land every 'Armistice Day'
Politicians and generals, with medals on display.
Make sure that they are well to the fore,
Unlike what they do when the guns roar.

The land fit for heroes, for which men died,
Did very little, for those who survived.

Thomas Boyle

VE DAY 1995

What do you recall of the war Granda?
What facts stick out in your mind?
Do you remember the Bombers?
The wake of destruction behind?
What did you see in the mornings?
Was there any hope left when they'd gone?
What were your thoughts at the time Granda?
Did you feel scared and alone?

No! My son. Never alone,
Never no hope for the few,
Never a doubt that my God would prevail,
Never a fear for the true.

What when the buildings were burning?
What as the siren spread fear?
What for the young and the injured?
What for the danger severe?
What where there wasn't a ration?
What when you couldn't find friends?
What when it seemed little mercy?
Looking at War with no end!

God finds a place for the starving,
God gives the suffering rest,
God in his mercy will judge friend or foe,
Those who are just will be blessed.

What did you do in the war Granda?
Did you have to stare death in the face?
Where are your scars of the battle?
Have they vanished, not leaving a trace?
What was your very worst moment?
What scared you more than the rest?
What was the fear in your heart at that time?
What, of all times, was your best?

I faced no more death than the next man,
My scars are the harm that was done,
My worst time was knowing that souls had been lost,
My best! . . . That the battle was won.

M J Stirling

TOGETHER FOR VICTORY

Fifty years or so, looking back at life
In war-time Britain; long years of strife
With no street lights, houses dark at night,
Blackout at each window, no chink of light.
Sirens blare out, street wardens alert -
'Go to the shelters lest you get hurt.'
Underground ones packed out every night,
Families together, safe from Hitler's might,
From shrapnel raining down, bombers overhead.
Our brave airmen fight in our stead.
It seems all London's burning, fires light the sky,
Firemen, workmen, police all hurrying by
To quench the flames, rescue those buried, in pain.
Strong hands dig them out; calls come again and again,
As they hope to hear an answering voice
And toil all night; there's no other choice,
Though some are beyond help. Weeks, months go by.
'How long ere peace comes?' We ask. As yet there's no reply,
But we hope it's soon. Nurses and doctors here and abroad
Work helping the wounded; no one can afford
To slacken their efforts until war is won,
And we can say to each other, ''twas a job well done.'

Vera Graver

THE VISION

I woke up this morning
And didn't know my name!
Stripped of all my worldly goods -
I didn't feel no shame . . .

High up on a mountain
Above the reach of sin . . .
I saw the world below me
And heard its awful din!

. . . I saw the battle of the Somme -
With all its bloody gore . . .

And horrors of the Atom-bomb
I hadn't seen before!

Then I heard a voice above -
I heard it loud and clear . . .
It told the story of Mankind,
And filled my soul with fear

People of each nation
Must learn to mend their ways,
Or trials and tribulations
Will shorten all their days!

Now I walk the city streets,
But are things what they seem?
Did a vision fill my soul . . .
Or was it just a dream?

Did a vision fill my soul . . .
Or was it just a dream?

Russell Humphrey

ANOTHER WAR

When I was young and in my prime
Before I knew the score
They trained me as a soldier
And sent me off to war

I travelled o'er the ocean
I discovered distant lands
I fought in bloody battles
Across the desert sands

When I was young and in my prime
With banners waving high
We fought a war to end all wars
And I watched people die

The battle cry was freedom
The world would be at peace
They sent us home as heroes
And so the fighting ceased

Now I am old and past my prime
I ask was it in vain
The world is in an uproar
Has it all come round again

How many wars to end all wars
How many killed and maimed
Will it go on forever
In man's search for power and fame

Again - young men and in their prime
Before they know the score
Are being trained as soldiers
And sent off to fight a war.

L Barnett

MIND THE DOORS PLEASE

I remember oh so well the horrors of the war,
When our brave boys came limping home, shell-shocked, maimed,
   foot-sore.
Did they receive the counselling for trauma and their fears?
No-way they just got on with life, and tried to stem their tears.

Those of us too young to fight, we lived from day to day
We learned to jive like GI Joe's before they sailed away
When the bombs came whistling down, *our* battle had begun
We dived into the underground and slept on platform one.

We tossed and turned as trains arrived, heard the coughs and snores
Just when you felt you're dropping off, a voice boomed
   'Mind the doors'
Bleary-eyed with lack of sleep, we climbed the stairs at dawn
Blinked like owls in sunlight and found our homes had gone.

We searched for all our treasured things in debris black and soggy
Thankfully the ARP had found our much loved moggy
If there is a God above please cancel World War III
I play 'Knock knock', *there's no reply*, the nation died you see!

Marion Lawson

SILENT TEARS

Silent tears;
unstoppable.
And sore hearts scream silently,
unechoed by invisible walls.

A grieving, inside, locked as deep
as if by prison chains.
Unseen by stranger's eye,
we cry.

Statistics jump out at them -
'Subhuman!'
But, foreigner, we're caught in war -
and who says war is human?

Frances McHugh

MONTE CASSINO

The shattered walls that stand, half-masted, to the sky;
The tangled threads of war; the blast-torn wire
That writhes o'er reeking rubble and desecrates the graves
Of those that rest beneath a common funeral pyre.
The myriad craters, laid to some inhuman plan, to form a Devil's links of countless holes,
Conceived by Satan, but the hazards wrought by man, ensnaring other poor benighted souls.
The empty cans and cartridge cases, spent in wanton waste; all flotsam on a sea of mud
That hold embroiled the flower of mortal youth that cannot blossom; failing e'en to bud.
The riddled hulls, half buried in piles of muck; or sunken in some shell-shot slimy pond:
The whole close grouped, impressive to extremes, and yet o'er shadowed by the hills and mangled Monastry beyond.
Mark this a resting place of men who conquered fear - or - being conquered, hid the fact in lies.
Build them no Cenotaph; there's one already here and consecrated, ''neath Italian skies.

Bernard Johnston

THE BLAMELESS MODERATE

I live in Northern Ireland
A country torn by strife
Where many have been left maimed
Where others have lost a life
I like to call myself a moderate
Who recognises the right of every man
Who detests the rioting and shooting
The flames of war I have no wish to fan
Yet am I so innocent that I do not feel
An anger that burnt in me like a flame
When someone I knew was shot or beaten
When they were without blame.
And do I not feel a hint of elation
When the other side are hit by grief
Is it because it was not one of ours again
Or is what I feel just a sense of relief
We all have different strengths
Our main instinct is to survive
There's safety in numbers
So we stand by our own
To try to stay alive
We talk of change and better laws
But when voting day comes around
We mainly vote the same ones in
Afraid of someone different who might threaten our tribal ground.
If someone was suffering
Because of civil war
Would I have courage and humanity to stop to help
Or carry on along my way as before
And if another's culture and politics
Are different from my own
Would I be as quick to point out injustice
Done to the other side and for them stand up alone
Does it matter so little to me
If a person is black, white, orange or green
Am I understanding and compromising enough

That their differences from me would be unseen
Am I so blameless? I don't help this country
When I can turn a blind eye
When I can utter an unkind word about another
Condemn the conduct of others with a sigh
To be just to others
Is for me an inward fight
To abate my animosity at times
I have to remind myself to respect another's right
To live differently from me
To worship and vote the way they like
And hope that we eventually will live in harmony
And overcome our differences and spite.

Ann McAreavey

WAR MEMORIAL

High on the cliff there stands a tall grey stone
The grey sea surging, breaking icy-white,
White flowers of foam dissolving in pale light.
About black rocks, the waves' perpetual moan.
The little birds to the warm south have flown;
Storm-clouds are gathering darkly on the height;
Red sunset dies into advancing night
That blurs the names engraved on the worn stone.
Wind swirls thin crimson petals on the tide;
The wheeling seagulls coldly cry above;
Unreal this place, these names, no longer known.
Lord, crucified forever, such your love,
God, who in suffering knew, the death those died,
Guide the lost world your love can save alone.

Diana Momber

TRIESTE - 1945

Maria and Ileana
The Contessa and the Archduchess
Were young volunteer nurses
At the 83rd Field Hospital
While Michael and I were patients

Later
They helped us at the youth club
On Piazzale Duca degli Abruzzi
As we struggled with the Scugnizzi
Under the hot Mediterranean sun

Afterwards
We four swam off Barcola
Their patrician skin
Had a bloom like peach velvet
And was the colour of ripe wheat
They even tasted burnt

In the evenings Maria
Would drop liquid
Into her eyes
They became luminous and mesmerising
As I watched

She stared into the mirror
As if by staring
She could learn something hidden
As her face
Became porcelain under the light

We ate fruita de mare
Cooked in olive oil
Served with cress
And we talked of love and
Her husband - the POW in Canada

She was a wild untamed
Volpe
She was the sun
And the South
Below the Alps - in war ravaged Italy

John W Dossett-Davies

A KLIC TOO FAR

He watches, waits, sixth sense probing, probing the blackness within his soul
The veneer of civilisation is stripped, nature's predator bared, exposed
Surviving that green hell, nerves shot, raw, his work taking its toll
More animal than man primeval urges forcing sanity's doors forever closed.

He lays motionless, listening, scenting his prey
Body tense, eyes narrowed his blade ready, impatient, craving the fight
His victims dispatched coldly, efficiently, left where they lay
Shadow-like he blends, melts into the jungle's heavy blanketing night.

Older now, withdrawn solitary, still playing, still in the hunt
A different playground, flashing lights, people, noise bouncing off concrete walls
he moves swiftly ignoring the crowds, eyes firmly on his target in front
One quick push, tyres screaming, horns blaring, he fades into the background as his victim falls.

Terry Bates

Blood Storm

The peacemakers sit comfortably
around a polished table
and talk with compassion
about the raging atrocities
in a land
torn apart by bloody war.

Listen the their
humane speeches
and realise that as each
word is uttered -
back in the fearful wasteland
of their concern,
snipers shoot children
playing in the streets -
men, women, children
and tiny babies
are slaughtered by mortar bombs
and people of a different faith
are exterminated
as the dark shadow
of the einsatzgruppen
falls on the earth.

Words, words, words
the deluge of words
dries up
and all the delegates
pose like statues
for the hungry cameras . . .

Yet no peace comes
as in the land drained of pity
survivors still cower in dark cellars
as the bloody talons
of hatred
claw down the innocent.

Stephen Gyles

SIXTEEN

I'm sixteen, one of three boys
Not long finished, playing with toys,
I'm sixteen , my passion is flowers
I've sat and studied them for hours.
I'm sixteen, and received my first letter
Addressed to, 'Mister Johnathan Petter,'
I'm sixteen, reporting for training
For twelve weeks, I'll be sweating and straining.
I'm sixteen, my first time on a boat
Nerves all taut, and a lump in my throat,
I'm sixteen, and march with the French
Into a field, into a trench.
I'm sixteen, I see a man die
It scared me so, I started to cry,
I'm sixteen, and have killed with a gun
For this is France, and I'm at Verdun.
I'm sixteen, and go 'over the top'
Where scores have fallen, keep going, don't stop,
I'm sixteen, and lie where poppies abound
In life's blood, oozing into the ground.
I'm sixteen, this can't be the plan
I died a boy, not yet a man.

Alan Charles

I Don't Want To Be Here

I know that they are in front of me, I crouch in sweat and fear,
The sergeant's voice behind me says 'There is the enemy at the rear.'
Perhaps if I lie low enough both will pass me by,
I don't want to be here, I don't want to die.

I can see the whites of his eyes - how did he get that near?
I really don't want to kill him and can see it's a thought we share.
Who will be the first to shoot or plunge a glistening knife?
Who will be the first to take the other's life?

Held rigid, suspended in the shock of sudden confrontation,
Hard breathing temporarily suspended in tense anticipation;
There has to be an outcome, neither can take flight,
My thoughts scream silently, this is not my war and certainly
                                                                not my fight.

Combat rages all around but an eerie silence fills my ears,
I want to be angry and aggressive but I feel compassion at his fears.
I can see his wife and family clearly reflected in his eyes -
One of us will leave a widow behind, if one of us survives.

A sudden shout, a shot, a dull and sickening thud,
Both of us wait to feel the pain or see the stain of blood.
My eyes are transfixed to his but there's no movement, none at all
Then his body sways and stumbles forward, and instinctively
                                                                 I break his fall.

It wasn't my gun that fired the shot that divested him of life,
It wasn't me that stopped him going home to family and wife.
I laid his body gently, sedately on the ground,
Oblivious of the war, the fighting and conflict all around.

Look after him God, take care of him, he was only doing a job
                                                                 like me.
Will all this hatred and violence really make men free?
If I ever get through this mess, youth will have passed me by -
I really don't want to be here, and I really don't want to die.

Jenny Chamberlain

THE TOYMAKERS

What thoughts fill the minds
Of those who devise
Modern merciless means of destruction?

At the mad moment of creation
Of such malevolent monsters
Mass murder must be the motivation.

Matters not that such missiles
Might never be employed,
The sin is established
At the moment of thought.

Suffering and extermination may follow,
For millions, for all mankind,
But what manner of evil lurks
At the moment of imagination
In the minds of the originators?

How far can they project their images
Beyond the clockwork efficiency
Of sadistic weaponry?

Repayment, not at the moment,
But in time momentous,
Will be the wages
Of those who conjure up
Such fiendish machinations
At the moment of thought.

Eric Allday

FLY BY NIGHTS?

Bombing up during the day. Engines tuned and chocks away.
Heavies lifting to the sky! Men intrepid as they fly!
Coastal crossing, o'er the sea. Flight path to the enemy!
Searchlights lighting up the sky entrapping bombers as they fly!
Bursting shrapnel from big guns, fired at you by the Huns!
Fighters zooming in to kill. This was not a flying thrill!
Colleagues, friends shot down in flames!
This was for real, not war games!
Target reached and bombsights aimed.
The 'load' discharged, direct hits claimed.
A turn for home one's duty done,
But still the fight through guns of Hun!
An engine hit, soon burning bright, lighting path for guns to sight
Weaving, dodging, losing height! A second engine hit this night.
Slowed down, coughing, flying low.
the pilot wrestles with airflow!
Navigator gives new course,
The coast is reached with great resource!
Then, skimming low over the waves,
Our crew take stock of their close shave!
Tail end 'Charlie's' lying dead. His lonely turret his deathbed!
Co-pilot's got a nasty wound but helps to keep the plane attuned!
The wings and tail are full of holes, all evidence of their patrol!
The fuel's low, gives cause for doubt!
Will we get home before it's out?
Old England's cliffs are barely cleared,
Strange aerodrome is reached.
A 'pancake' landing with no wheels, the pilot made a peach!
Another plane is written off, the cost to us is dear!
The planes and men lost every night give cause for rising fear!
But still they build! And still they fly! And bomb by day and night!
The enemy must be worn down and pounded out of sight!

What use the war? What victory won? At costs so very dear!
Destruction and the aftermath give little cause for cheer!
For those that lost, the total cost was never worth the start!
For those that won? A job well done! But with a heavy heart!

Deane Wynne

HE DIED A HERO

Triumphant were the songs on our return,
but inside our heads the horrors burned,
of stumbling through fear-laden nights,
to fight a politician's fight,
to scorch the earth and leave no trace,
to die with honour not disgrace,
to kill and maim and kill again,
the machine moves forward quite insane,
mortar shells fly overhead,
don't look back we know they're dead,
explosions on us and around,
our jets fly in and strafe the town,
the mortars now have silent fell,
those who survived survey this hell,
I stared into my best friend's eyes,
all that's left I could recognise,
'he died a hero' that's what they'll say,
no mention of his body blown away,
a mortar ripped his life apart,
and broke his family's hopeful heart,
so they're not here singing songs and waving flags,
they're home packing daddy's clothes in bags.

J Stanbury

As Was And Is

Come on my lads, the guns are hungry
Over the top, by the whistle,
Young Tom and Ted, Sid from the lane
Plus Roy from the Dog and Thistle.

The bayonets fixed, and rifles steady
The light of the morning is dull,
The mist on the ground is slowly thinning
Is time for old death's daily cull.

The cannons are roaring in falsified anger
Just time for a prayer, for long life,
And, perhaps, in the foot a slight blighty
Then leave to go home to the wife.

Now over the top, and steadily forward
One section of men with the rest,
A thick mass of khaki, officers waving
Walk crouched to the enemy's nest.

First fell young Tom, a look of surprise
On a face of soft youth and high dreams,
Death on the instant, all so unknowing
'Mid the far spread groans and loud screams.

Next with a crack, torn fire and smoke
Both Sid and Roy went as one,
Their space filled in seconds by others advancing
Going grey-faced to the Hun.

Ted was unlucky, his legs cut clean off
By blast from a short-fall shell,
His life ebbed away in a foreign land
As death took its passage through hell.

Soon, in the silence that followed the din
The day's dead and dying lay bleeding,
Making richer the soil that hard beneath
Leaving rivers of tears for the weeping.

So was, and is, the product of conflict
When innocent die for some reason,
When given no choice, but the fight then presented
And refusal to join called foul treason.

Henry J Green

JUST ONE WORD, WAR!

What happened yesterday?
What happened today?
Will it happen tomorrow . . . ?
I just dread to say!

Somewhere, one man with 'power'
Utters threats of *war*, to claim
land from another country
Sends troops to bomb and maim!

Killing weak and defenceless
There are battles, there is fear,
Homes, families, lives are lost
Destruction, death hovers near!

A scorched earth, devastation,
Screams and sobbing heard,
Young, old, animals all starving,
Because of just *one* word!

If,
No weapons, no bombs, no power
No *wars* no killing, and no fear,
No 'history repeats' anywhere in the world,
Utopia, heavenly peace would be here!

S M Bush-Payne

WE TAKE LIFE FOR GRANTED

Summertime, we sit in our gardens, and enjoy the sunshine.
Admire the flowers and plan for holidays,
we take life for granted

While somewhere abroad war is raging.
People huddled together in cellars and small rooms,
Bombs dropping and scattering houses and families to pieces,
People running and screaming for mercy.

While we take life for granted,
Going to work, doing our daily chores,
Grumbling because our bills are too high,
Or because something has gone wrong in our lives.

While somewhere abroad war is raging,
A broken-hearted mother leans over her dead baby crying.
Bodies everywhere, homes deserted,
Men, women and children, with their belongings, moving on.

While we take life for granted,
Going shopping, celebrating birthdays, anniversaries, and weddings,
Enjoying our homes, and being free to do what we like!

While somewhere abroad war is raging,
Heavy aircraft overhead with menacing noises of their engines,
Terrorising people, and destroying the land,
No water, no crops, no food, no hope. Just the stink of death.

While we take life for granted!
That is, until it is our turn!
We must not take life for granted!

Eda Singleton

NOT FORGOTTEN

There among the ruins
of that humble cottage home
There where spiders hung their webs
Spider webs in every room.
Little furniture was left
a table in the hall
There the remains of a candle
That shone on a picture
a picture that still hung on the wall
picture of a soldier medals in a row
how they shone in candlelight
All those years ago.
left but not forgotten
Brave men still live on.

Golden letters beneath the picture
read
'He gave his life for his
friend
Killed in action
Helping a comrade'

Battle of the Somme
July 18, 1916
'A supreme sacrifice'
John.

Frances Gibson

A POINT OF VIEW

Why should we mourn for those
Bright stars that fall through war?
Their laughing youth has died,
The left loved ones have cried.

Why should we mourn for those?
Their deaths a blaze of light,
Their names writ on the sky,
Why should the loved ones cry?

Why should we cry indeed
To hold those youthful stars?
How can we see ahead
The life they might have led?

How do we know that life
Will be a rosy path,
With all their dreams come true
And skies perpetual blue?

How do we know? We don't.
(My ways are not your ways)
We only hope the years
Will not be filled with tears;

The cancer's growing rot
The mind shell-shocked, blind eyes.
Is this what we foresaw
And wished them evermore?

What do we know of minds
Tormented, knowing hell?
Seeking and searching peace
Or wishing life would cease.

Before we wish them life
And mourn, think for a spell;
Shall sadness, worries, strife
Shall these affect their life?

Surely a life cut short
In its rich prime and joy
Before regrets and sighs
Can gather as time flies.

Surely such shining life
Unspoiled and fresh and new
Shall give, inspire and lead
The lives, that they have freed?

Therefore let us not mourn,
Rather rejoice that they
Are free from fates queer twists
And ages creeping mists.

R Garrett

FERTILE FIELDS

The fertile minds lie buried
In far-off lands
Of men who, in their valiant way
Tried to halt aggression
And for freedom
Paid with their lives

These fields, now harvested each year
Have the seeds of hope and promise
Though watered with many an uncontrollable tear
Reaching for life so precious
We must find
A less destructive answer
For the problems of mankind!

Tamar Segal

COLOGNE
(Reflections over the Rhine)

It's peaceful now, the sky is clear,
The evening sun is sinking low -
Casting shadows o'er the Rhine
And grapes are ripening on the vine.
yet listen hard and you may hear
The drone of bombers from long ago,
When Bomber Command
Rode the dangerous sky
Wreaking havoc on those below.

'Bombs gone Skipper'
'Goodbye Cologne.'
But so many never made it home!
Oblivion immediate
When blown from the sky,
or extended awareness
Of rapid descent;
In time but two minutes,
Eternal in length.

Mind confused with tracers glare,
Still hearing the screams -
'A Messerschmitt' - 'Where?'
'Port quarter up - coming in fast'
'Corkscrew - corkscrew - I'm hit.'
'My turret's on fire' -
'Help - someone help me' -
Then silence at last:
And from high overhead -
A Lancaster fell past.

Half a century's gone by,
The air crews who survived
Are feeling their years;
Have grown grey haired and old:
But those gallant young airmen
In memories remain;
Immortal - still here!
Suspended in time -
Above Cologne: above the Rhine.

Peter Marshall

THE PRISONER OF WAR

As a prisoner of war, I led an unusual life,
With days of hunger, and hours of strife,
Existing somehow, surrounded by wire,
Withstanding the cold, without any fire,
The shortage of food, made life very tough,
The small daily ration, was never near enough.

Three times a day, they provided a drink,
Supposed to be coffee, and what do you think?
We gave it a name, that caused quite a giggle,
T'was always referred to, as some sort of piddle,
Each day came spuds, with their jackets on,
They must have grown them, by the tone.

Five of us shared, one loaf of bread,
Just a small loaf, and as heavy as lead,
The soup, called 'skilly,' was thin, but always hot,
A pint of that, was my daily lot,
The Red Cross parcel, was our only friend,
Which kept me going, until the end.

Bert Richings

THOUGHTS OF WAR

The old man said 'In God's name why?'
and again 'In God's name why?'
Down the rugged cheeks of his wizened face
a tear ran from his eye.

'My wife and son, my dearest son
my greatest pride and joy,
cut down in the prime of life good sir
and he yet still a boy.

His mother too, Lord rest her soul
and here he gave a shudder,
they shot her first then shot our son
as he lay in the arms of his mother.

'Twas the war kind sir, the hellish war
that took away my lover,
and with her too my only son
who died in the arms of his mother.'

With piteous voice now racked with sobs
and with eyes now raised to heaven,
'A curse on those who killed my wife
and my darling son aged seven.'

Mike Coyle

OLD AND YOUNG

The old are glorious. Old buildings
bringing us the past. Old trees
with all the life they carry. Old people
rich with memories. All these are glorious.
But where is glory in
a building bombed, a broken tree,
a body that was never let grow old?

The young are glorious. Young flowers
splash the world with hope. Young homes
where glad new families can grow. Young people
playing in the street. All these are glorious.
But where is glory in
wilting wreaths, burning homes
and heroes who have hardly tasted life?

Fred Brown

NOT ON MY STREET

A radio operator alerts a driver of a pick-up,
Another fare to help pay the rent,
Unbeknown to anyone but the perpetrator,
He is about to die,
No one from that address has ordered a taxi,
Only blood is to be spent.

It is a set up,
Callously shot at point blank range,
Another senseless killing,
Another family plunged into mourning,
The world of the radio operator falls apart,
She cannot yet her feelings of despair assuage.

Where could this happen?
Surely war happens in lands far away and remote,
Not on my doorstep!
Not on my street!
The report comes from Belfast,
It's a recent anecdote.

Mary Brackley

THE KILLING FIELDS

In the stillness grow the poppies
Where they never grew before
Fed and nurtured by the blood
of the fallen, in the First World War
Tended now with loving care
The graves of those that fell
in the battles won, and battles lost
amidst the terrible shot and shell
And what of those that also died
in the infamous holocaust
Who knew nothing of their fate
Just their ashes spread like dust
Six million souls gave up their lives
To satisfy the power-mad few
A terrible, needless waste also
of the nation called the Jew
No known graves have these poor souls
No poppies for them will flower
But none will ever be forgotten
As we remember all, at the eleventh hour
Forget not, the indiscriminate minefields
laid down to maim and kill
left there to do their deadly work
Are they not, 'The killing fields still'.

C O Desjarlais

DIARY OF WAR

They sent them out to face the guns.
'Come on lads' they cried.
'For King and country do your bit,'
And in the mud they died.

1914

'We need you,' claimed the posters.
'Come on, do your bit.
Leave your farms and villages,
Show a bit of grit.'

1915

Lives were not important
As the generals made their moves.
Young blood was expendable
And they died in droves.

1916

Brother next to brother,
Over the top at dawn.
Barbed wire, machine guns
And mothers left to mourn.

1917

When the guns fell silent
And a man could take a breath,
Hellish gas came creeping
And the cool wind brought him death.

1918

It was a war to end all wars
Was the oath to crippled men.
But well within their lifetime
We went to war again.

Eileen Boden

SOCIETY DOESN'T CARE

Moving pictures on my TV screen, remind me what's going on in the world
Homelessness, famine, war, are just a few I mention
I scold myself for being so materialistic, for wanting things that others would regard as luxuries.
I never had a proper family, these people did, they had to watch them die, they too have become orphans.
I decide each day, what to eat, these people have no choice, for some there is no food for days.
For them there are no birds singing, no blue skies.
The only noise they hear is the constant gunfire, the screaming.
Their blue skies are painted with smoke, their trees have been destroyed.
Our country may not be perfect, but at least together we can make it into something we desire
These people have no choice.
Society has to start caring, not just in our own country, but in theirs.
Peace has to be made, for the sake of the thousands who are suffering.
Along with all the nations, governments and independent people,
We have to start caring.

Ann Willbourne

WHO WILL TELL?

Who will tell my family
When I am dead and gone?
Who will tell my family?
That I their only son

Went off to war with boys like me
To march and fight across the sea
Shoulder to shoulder they lay as they fell
Bad news for families someone must tell.

These men for me became my brothers

Who spoke their love and cried for mothers
We were so young and bravely bold
As we marched along within the fold.

Who will tell my family
When I too am dead and gone
Who will tell my family
About me their loving son.

B Tully

A Survivor Of War

A bomb exploded, his eyes darted to the sound
He looked, there was devastation all around
Was this his country all the time at war
Never any peace what was all this fighting for
All the miles they had trekked to stay alive
Knowing they may have to leave as soon as they arrive
He was thinking is this what they call life?
Politicians argue, but in reality it's a tribal strife
Painful memories of his family gone
When he becomes a man, would it still be going on
His shelter leaked every time it rained
Without the help of the Red Cross it was a strain
How well he remembered the words of his Dad
This war would go on till the country was sad
But he always knew the thing to do
Keep surviving and he'd come through
Surely in the end they'd see the light
Then end the war, and end the fight.

H Fox

THE NIGHT LONDON WAS ABLAZE

Anxiety neurosis they called it,
But I had good cause,
Hadn't I?
Searchlights on a September evening,
Enemy aircraft overhead
The Luftwaffe delivering bombs
As I stood in a doorway
Alone.
Parents with friends
Not knowing
In spite of my unheard cries.
Sitting in an earthen shelter
Shaking
Just waiting to die.
Mouth tight and dry
This is where my stomach
Learned to grip and twist
In torturous
Knots.
Mother, father, brothers, sister
Somewhere else
I knew not where?
Grandparents trying to calm,
But knowing the awful
Truth.
This is not
The ideal beginning
For an infant
To form
Stability
Security
Hope.

L J Culbert

DON'T STOP TRYING

I love laying by your side, it makes my pulse and
                                                  my heart race
When I look carefully at your relaxed and
                                                  smiling face
Your lovely sparkling eyes remind me of shining
                                                  stars in the sky
And your tongue brushes your lips because your
                                                  lips are dry.

I love to fiddle with your hair, it makes my
                                                  pulse race
The adrenaline is pumping at an extraordinary
                                                  pace
You catch me watching you and gently kiss
                                                  my lips
I'm getting a funny tingle in my toes and finger
                                                  tips

We are always together, we're inseparable you
                                                  and I
And our precious time together always seems to
                                                  fly
No sooner are you by my side then it's time to
                                                  go
Earlier we were happy but now we're both feeling
                                                  low

Our love grows even stronger, it matures day
                                                  after day
Somehow we overcome the hurdles that seem to
                                                  get in our way
We never ever argue, and we never ever fight
We will always be together because we keep our
                                                  love alight.

Deborah Butcher

WAR TIME

My brother, grasp both clock hands
And turn them, forwards,
Quickly, do not spare a second
To be complacent or doubtful,

For war and time
Are inextricably linked
And I cannot, must not, live
In an era of destruction
Where lives are lost
For nothing,

I know the pain of sorrow
May harsh times escape me,
I am not weak-willed or a coward
May cold actions, and cruelty
pass me by,

My brother, take both my hands
And turn my palms outwards,
Turn them to face the sky
Comfort me and be patient.

Liam St Clair

PEACE OR WAR?

The tender shoot of peace,
Long-nurtured,
Lies uprooted, frail, down-trodden.
By heels of ruthless men.

The cruel streak of hate
Deep-hidden.
Rises, awakened, fed and nourished
By hate and greed of men.

The strong thread of hope,
Unbroken,
Stays undaunted, safe, secure
In hearts of Christian men.

W L Oakley

THE POPPIES REMEMBER...

The poppies sway in the gentle breeze
recalling days gone by.
Days when all the meadows saw
was guns, blood and distress.
None of the soldiers did realise
the horror that lay ahead
they'd heard of what could happen
but no, it wouldn't to them.
Then gradually it happened
to strangers, and their friends
The pain to watch loved ones die
was almost too much to bear.
The soldiers were brave
fighting on to the end
their duty was to their country
But what was the point
in those bitter wars?
Countries should just live in peace.
Innocent people lost their lives
and families were destroyed.
Many people have now forgotten
but the poppies' memory lives on ...

Gemma Titchener (14)

DEATH WISH

There are not enough dead,
Not enough dying.
Not enough children
Killed on the roads
Every day.

Not enough needless deaths
Not enough mothers
In childbirth
Not enough middle-aged daddies
Dying at home from heart attacks
In hospital from cancer.

Doctors are curing too many people.
Doctors are overworking
At weekends in hospitals.
A trip to the mortuary to see
Stare at successful suicides
Won't show
Enough dead.

Not enough drownings on coastal beaches
On bank holidays.
Not enough people trapped in fires
Nor bodies covered in burns.

Not enough needless death.
Diseases are doing their best.
Accidents are trying hard.
But we aren't careless enough
About squashing other people's squelchy bodies
Too squeamish.

Not enough murders
On the front pages of newspapers.
Hangings
Are quite out of fashion.

Not enough bombs in supermarkets.
Bring death in, off the streets
Into the homes.
Every home should have one.
Let's have a riot of death.

Just not enough death to go round.
Every family needs a couple of deaths.
Not enough old people dying,
Not enough young people dying.
Let's have more young people dying.

If we train all our young men
For two years
To kill
That should be enough
Our army might make enough
Dead
Nearly enough.

Angela Lansbury

WARS FADE

War, war, wars
Many question the cause
Still victory enforced
Though unease falls over war
Conquer with bloodstained hands
Human price over land
Memory of death remains instead
Future settlement minus bloodshed
Wars fade as peace makes way
Humanity hopes and prays.

Alan Jones

SOME MOTHER'S SON

Dear Mother I write this letter
As daylight disappears
As pictures of blood and battle
Are lost for a few precious hours.

The sound of the guns and rockets
Will continue all through the night
But our vision is thankfully lessened
The carnage exchanged for starlight.

Do these same stars watch over you
Their nightly vigil to keep
Do you wonder if I'm looking at them
Before you drift off to sleep.

Perhaps you don't dwell so deeply
When their absolute wonder is shown
As your son here, in the battle does
Lost, frightened, alone.

Will I ever see my home again
Will I walk with you awhile
Gaze up at those same heavens
As I did when yet a child.

This war was not of our making
We did not choose the fight
And yet our country sent us
To help another's plight.

They shoot at us, we shoot at them
By our Captains we are led
And in between the innocents
Are maimed, crushed left for dead.

I am cold, hungry, dirty
Feeling at life's low ebb
Wondering, what we're doing here
When will this conflict end.

I look up to the stars again
How futile this all seems
This world will not stop turning
Just for a madman's dream.

We're here to satisfy someone's greed
Their longing for power and fame
While we, the soldiers, perish
And are left in a foreign grave.

I may not see tomorrow's stars
Or even tomorrow's light
So Mother just in case it's so
I whisper, goodbye, night night.

For always down through all the years
Where wars are fought and won
The final sacrifice has been
Some poor Mother's son.

Joy Nethercot

BALKAN RHAPSODY

Our oneness torn apart forever
For the sake of national pride
Shifting frontiers just to sever
What was never felt inside

We are invaded by an uncivil war
Cleansed by our ethnic neighbours right through
And the west keeps an eye on the score
United Nations can't unite on their view

While the Danube is choked with our tears
For the loved ones we can never forget
Passing seasons can't allay our fears
Our sorrow our heartache our regret.

Charlie Maunsell

PEACE

For the peace that is written in a baby's eyes,
Stop the wars,
Crush not the flowers, their glory is ours,
And all because
Our Saviour willed it so.

Cloud not the sun with the smoke of battle,
No battle is ever won,
They can only be losers who hurt God's creatures
And cloud the warmth of the sun.

For the wars that have been, may the wounds start to heal,
As we think of the Saviour who died on a cross,
And remember the pain His hands would feel,
Let it be a blessing, not a loss.

Think of a world, how it could be
With no one walking in fear,
Think of a world that has no war,
Let us act and it could be here.

With peace in our hearts, with quiet hands,
We can build a world of love, it's true,
The prince of Peace gave His life for this,
A world of beauty for me and you.

Hilary Mason

A Brief History Of War

The Greeks and the Persians
are at war.
The Romans and the Carthaginians
settling old scores.

The Normans beat the Britons
for a new land,
Then they went to Palestine
influenced by God's hand.

Portugal fought against Spain
for precious golden cargo,
And France battled Europe
for one man's ego.

Japan fought against China
with great bloodshed,
Then Germany fought the world
for the demons in a man's head.

The Americans went to Vietnam,
many sons were lost.
The Soviets invaded Afghanistan
at such great cost.

Iraq took on Kuwait,
one man's insanity.
Yugoslavia imploded into many small pieces
for this is humanity.

Daniel R Deakin

THE EVACUEE

His mother took him on her knee
And spoke these words tremulously
'Remember I love you come what may'
'But tomorrow morning you'll be going away'

She told of air-raids yet to come
Expected from the dreaded Hun
From fear of those she did decree
He was to become an evacuee

Tears brought dimness to his eyes
'Be brave' she said, 'little boys don't cry'
She held him close and smoothed his hair
He sensed her feeling of deep despair

She rocked him gently to and fro
Seemingly never wanting to let him go.
Words of encouragement to him she gave
'Your father would want you to be brave.'

A picture of his father stood
On the mantleshelf - framed in wood
There in battle dress he stood proud
He looked toward, then said aloud

'Don't worry Mom, I shall be alright
I will write you a letter every night'
With those words it was then she cried
From emotion she could no longer hide.

So the following morning, hand in hand
They met and joined a growing band
Of lined up children - lines of threes
All set to become evacuees.

To Waterloo Station they were led
As they boarded the train 'Goodbyes' were said
Through the windows, little heads were poked
Waving to mothers whose throats were choked.

He never saw his mother again
She was killed in an air-raid - his age was 10
A short while later his uncle came
(His father had been killed at El Alamein).

50 years have passed on by
Lost in memory he will sometimes cry
With nostalgia he becomes engrossed
And grieves for the parents that he loved and lost.

J Newman

GREEN FIELDS

The old soldier's wounds may have healed
but his thoughts might often dwell
on the crimson hue
he saw in the battlefield.

On Remembrance Day we wear a poppy
blood red
in case we forget the dead,
and at the Cenotaph we stand
head bowed low
and we listen in silence
to the bugles blow
and sadness fills our heart.

The killing fields are a scarlet
chapter from the past
but we don't want the green fields
tinged with red in Belfast.

Iris Kelly

LETTER

I opened up the letter
Tears did fill my eyes
My son, my first born's writing
I was holding in my hands.

I smelled the letter over
To try and get a trace of him
The one I love so much
I need to see his face.

I could picture deserts
With tents all pegged down tight
Bareness all around
Would fill your hearts with fright.

To all the politicians!
Don't make no sense to me
War is such an ugly word
But then they must be free.

Captive ones I think about
I prayed for you today
So you would all be free
And with your family stay.

Tension now is mounting
Won't someone make a stand?
Saddam, it's up to you - please
Don't force their hand.

Think of all your people.
Yes both young and old
And all the fine ones fighting
If war were to unfold.

Pause for just a little while . . .
What the cost will be
In lives I'm talking now
And not of oil, agree!

They say I'll be a grandma
In just a little while
I want to see my son's face light with pride
And then I'll smile.

To see a new life beginning
The greatest gift of all
So a plea I'll make today
Don't start this bloody war!

S Hine

CROSS-FIRE OR THE CROSS?

Blood-bathed babe - innocence -
Who are the victims of war?
The innocents! War is raw.
Who is the enemy?
What is the uniform or insignia?

The beginning may be from the comfort
Of the politician's plush chair.
The ending will be a 'killing field' - perhaps Zaire.
Echoes of war remain the same -
Seek - kill - maim!

What a waste! Wounds and blood-taste.
Blood-bathed babe; such innocence
Is worth everything.
War is futile! Humanity is on the brink
Of extinction.
Cover the bayonet! Blunt the bullet!
Politicians . . . please think!

R Peter Smith

FAR BEYOND A WORLD A MAN WEEPS!

Tomorrow, we may never see.
As we are in a war of killing fields.
Torment of what our lives have become.
Blameless of innocence
Justice, we don't see.
Men - we hear crying in pain.
A hand reaches out but, who can help when
you're dying yourself.
Oh, no comfort, no dignity.
Darkness shadows over us.
Hurt, torment of destruction of war.
Our eyes close for the last time.
Far beyond a world.
A man weeps,
Tomorrow, we may never see.
As we are in a war of killing fields.

Claudia

AFRICA AGAIN

Once again Africa is in the headlines.
Another power struggle full of senseless carnage.
Rapes, beatings and atrocities,
The consequence of man's inhumanity.
Time and opportunity to settle grievances that have been restrained,
Now they are unleashed and out of control.
We see the children wandering alone, shocked and dazed.
Orphaned, who will hold and care for them?
Are we immune to their pain?
After all 'it's only Africa again'!
Would it matter if the child was white instead of black?

Joy Aldridge

LITTLE WHITE CROSSES

Little white crosses standing in rows
Was it really worth it? Who knows?

On the road to Paris from Calais
There is a lot to remind you of war.
As you leave the beaches of Normandy
Drive through the Somme and Picardy
Names that have come down the years
With memories, of loved ones, tears.
Little white crosses standing in rows,
Was it really worth it, who knows?

Woods lie on either side
Where no birds sing, the warm earth
Covering those who lie where they fell
Fighting on either side for whatever reason
Their names still unknown. For them not even
Little white crosses standing in rows,
Was it really worth it, who knows?

The road to Paris is open to all
Green are the fields where children play
Laughter is heard, not gunfire and shells.
Theirs is the future so costly won.
Playing so freely beneath the sun.
Little white crosses standing in rows
They make it worth it. God knows!

Polly Bennison

A KILLING FIELD

Was it in Cambodia or Vietnam
That the killing field began?
Or was it in England's green and pleasant land
Where scientists gave out a helping hand?
Not with land mine nor with gun,
But something silent, helped by rain and sun.
The connoisseur could not define
Why no dandelions grew to make sweet wine.
Then the children's special flowers
killed in minutes not in hours;
Fumbling fingers never again
To make a necklace with a daisy chain,
No buttercup held beneath a chin
To make children smile and grown-ups grin.
No gun nor bullet nor land mine,
Science took another line
Something that they tried to hide
The very deadly pesticide.

D W Owen

WHEN WAR WILL BE NO MORE

Oh you politicians
Oh you men of war
Why don't you remember
What life is really for?

No mothers' sons should have to lie
In filthy trenches, where they die,
Man wasn't born to kill each other
Whatever their creed, or what their colour.

Life should be about loving and living,
Helping each other and forgiving.
Not about bullets and killing
For there are no winners in war,

So all you politicians
All you men of war
In the next millennium
Make sure peace will always score.

M A Atkinson

CASUALTIES OF WAR

Why are women and children sighing,
What are they all waiting for,
Wringing their hands and crying,
Because their men have gone to war,
Away in a foreign land,
Far from the ones they love,
Marching over burning sands,
Hot and weary with every move.
Bombs falling from the air,
Guns firing on the ground,
They ask 'Does no-one care?'
As their ears burst with the sound,
Fathers, sons and husbands dying,
Their bodies, stiff and still.
That is why there's so much crying,
Why do men need to kill?

J E Simpkins

The Soldier

Close my eyes and let me sleep,
Before the dreams begin to seep
Into my consciousness,
And fill my mind with hideousness,
Peacefully let me lie
Until the morning sun I spy,
And gladly greet the day
Which blows the foul night away.
Why do such dreams arise,
Twisted thoughts that terrorise,
Across the regions of the night,
Horror upon horror affright;
Before I reach perdition
Send me your physician,
Let him reach into my head
And kill these black evils dead,
Take away this terrible dread,
Give me sunshine thoughts instead.
When did I begin to live this sin,
What devilish tricks have I been in,
Unsought, unknowing,
These monsters have been growing,
From cavernous depths within my head,
But, now watch me with this gun,
And tiny piece of lead,
Kill them dead.

I Vincent

COLD

Scattered amongst the ruins of my mind
    The innocent dress of day is war torn.
A colourless grey landscape is circled
    By a charcoal city
Where cold metal flowers protrude to poison the soul.
    Each side believes in God,
As Satan laughs at a life given for devils in the red of blood.
    Silence of death is washed all around
Mocking the already grim atmosphere,
    Crowding the crooked air with the gas of disaster.

Memories of trees are as unreal as dreams of freedom,
    The smell of decay lingers with the darkness
As time's evil face denies everything
    As it strikes its merciless wrath of silence.
Beyond the shadow of shadows
    Lies the river of frozen beliefs,
Cold and unforgiving, bitter stale, bitter stale
    She sends her treachery
To an even deeper goal
    Filling with more political sewers.

The cry of a mother without child
    Breaks into the agony
Like a saw screaming against metal,
    Merciless and embittered, oiled to perfection
Into ruthless military mission of destruction.
    Here they mourn the living, take from the hand of God
Lying frozen to the ground is a dove of white,
    Fired from the heavens, - forever
To remind us that inside the tombstone
    Is indeed the gates of God . . .

And we continue to sew our words of peace into the killing fields . . .

Charles Thomson

THE MESSAGE

Why cause all this pain - stop the fighting, let peace come again.
Let children live within their homes,
With loving parents to guide.
Tell all the soldiers to lay down their guns,
There is no need to hide.
Fear can go, trust will return,
No more fighting - no villages to burn,
The long summer days, we welcome them anew,
The lovely green fields and skies of blue.
Friendships will remain and new ones will be made
Now the war is over, because of prayers we prayed.
Tomorrow is a new day,
From now on life starts again,
We are the future -
Past mistakes have caused too much pain.

Barbara Froggatt

THE BANQUET

Etched into their tombstones,
on every grain of sand.
The hallmark of the Devil,
the footprint of the damned.
The Exocet, the shrapnel,
the fear that tears the mind,
the battlefield's a banquet on
which the Devil has richly dined,
the menu is the soldier boy
that fate as blindly planned,
to march into oblivion in
the footprints of the damned.

B J Jones

EVACUATED

Tear stained infant
tagged for travel,
nose pressed on railway carriage window.
Mummy,
where are you?

Grim faced strangers
old but willing,
waiting for their piece of human baggage.
Mummy,
I want you.

Bedroom, lamp-lit,
windows draped black,
every corner home to ghosts and wolves.
Mummy,
I'm frightened.

Weeks, then months,
then years of waiting,
wondering when the train will take me home.
Mummy,
I miss you.

Peal of church bells
hailing victory.
Back to things familiar once, now strange.
Daddy,
where are you?

M Hume

EVERY ONE A MOTHER'S SON

He saw the storm clouds gathering
He heard the nationalistic rantings
He felt deep patriotic leanings
He spoke in support
He knew the conflict would soon begin

He saw the posters demanding recruitment
He heard the marching feet of many
He felt elation that he would play a part
He spoke of the glory he would share
He knew they would triumph

He saw the enemy on the horizon
He heard the crump of the distant guns
He felt a wave of elation soak his body
He spoke with enthusiasm to his comrades
He knew he was ready

He saw destruction arrive with a vengeance
He heard screams that assaulted his ears
He felt the earth move erupting around him
He spoke little of glory or gain
He knew that fear now ruled and controlled him

He saw darkness descend on his aura
He heard rushing from inside his brain
He felt pain at the root of his being
He spoke screams from depths of his throat
He knew it was the beginning of the end

He now could not see any beauty
He would never again hear the wind
He felt life draining out all around him
He spoke words that no longer had sound
He knew he was dead

He saw the gentle face of the Madonna
He heard the loving tone of her voice
He felt the warmth of her breast where he suckled
He spoke with eyes that beheld her in love
He knew who she was.

T D Watson

STOP THINK

All of you and all of us are responsible
for our actions.
Take a long hard look into the mirror,
and say it does not matter, (it's not us)
      It does.
Put down your arms, think before
we all sink each and everyone of us
      into oblivion.
Let us show the next generation
how life could be.
Without the need to fight,
to never ever run again,
or be frightened of the night.

Take a look into a child's eyes
See their pain, you have caused,
it is surely all you need to know.
Their grief could be gone forever
If it wasn't for these bloody wars.
Wipe away their tears,
Wipe out the wars
      forever.
But how?

Kathleen Scarborough

BELFAST...

I often wonder how it feels,
For the men who did those dastardly deeds,
Do they dull their minds with a pint of beer?
Can they sleep in their beds, without any fear?
The sad empty homes, this Christmastide,
Bereft of fathers, mothers and child,
Where is my daddy the young boy cries?
Too young to remember, the tragic night,
The gunmen entered his happy home,
And killed his daddy, who died alone.
'Mistaken identity', the headlines read,
While his wife and children, buried their dead,
Dear God, in your mercy, comfort them all,
Bring peace to their hearts, is my fervent call.

Bernadette Kennedy

FLAGS AND TEARS

Uniformed men wearing helmets
carrying guns and shields.
Primed for battle;
Silent faceless men carrying guns and bombs
Destroyers of life and limb
Weeping women fatherless children
Maimed limbs, dead bodies;
Coffins wrapped in flags
People wrapped in grief;
Their tears are not coloured.
Unlike their shared Christianity
Stained red by shed blood
Are the Lord's tears rainbow hued?

M T Breslin

BORDERLINE

A single gunshot rattles,
Across a deserted street,
Empty caverns of houses,
Where two borders meet.

A single soldier watches,
In the wreck of someone's home,
Beady eyes on the borderline,
In case the enemy should roam.

A single thought floats,
Within the soldier's head,
Of the first man,
He ever shot dead.

A single tear falls,
Down his dirty face,
Wanting to be home,
Instead of this killing place,

A single wish forms,
Of the futility of war,
As he sits cramped and tired,
And wonders what it's for.

A single gunshot rattles,
Across the silent street,
Soldiers' minds devoid of thought,
Where two borders meet.

M Mickley

TOMMY

Our Tommy stood there waiting
In the dank and muddy trench
Bayonet fixed onto his rifle
Waiting for the final order
Ready for the next charge,
He turned to his mate,
'Gizza light me owd duck
it might be me last fag.'
His mate lit up with him
They puffed on their fags
Then down came the signal
And over the top they went
Shouting loud their war cries
Into the blazing enemy guns
But it was in vain, dropping
onto the already reddened soil,
Tommy fell with the others
Yes it was his last fag,
His name will be on a monument,
A tall concrete folly
The folly of all mankind.
Will it ever end?
Will it ever cease?
These futile wars of man
One day perhaps, one day.

David Brownley

IT WASN'T ME

'It wasn't me' he muttered,
when the majority of voters
mistakenly placed a crossed slip
in a ribboned box, 'It wasn't me'
when the tail-gating traffic was
smashed to ribbons on a motorway, with
a cavalcade of injured and dead, and
wreckage strewn to the horizon.

'It wasn't me' when a death spray,
praised in shrieking advertisement,
killed off nature, and sent men writhing
in agony to the surgeries.

It wasn't him when countries were
desecrated by conflict, where innocent
civilians, packed in hordes, were
massacred for ethnic reasons, not
qualified in law. It wasn't him when
the dead were chiselled out of the
earth for evidence, and when, nearer
to home, the bones of mediaeval time
were bulldozed out for development
profiteers to create a concrete jungle.

It wasn't him when a motorway was
slashed through woodland, thousands
of years in its evolution, making a
mockery of truth and advocacy, it wasn't
him, but it was somebody like him.

Richard Ball

Last Christmas

I am sitting here alone
In this cold, cold, bolted cellar,
Swallowing the last of the port,
And groping for the panatellas
Which a late friend sent me;
Trying to remember
The Christmas cards
Somewhere in the dining room, perhaps,
Which I dare not go and look for.

The turkey, in its body bag,
Rots in the windy kitchen,
And is more fortunate,
Being strangled just in time.
And there will be no sparrows
To peck the pudding's crumbs;
It will be a billion years
Till beaks and cartons.

I learned the insanity
Of courage now,
(After the laying on of fingers),
When on Christmas Day, I think,
I crept outside,
And saw sculptured shadows,
And possibly children,
And skimmed juggernauts across a piece of Mars,
And swatted jets,
And looked in vain
For tower blocks and hills.
So I returned
To this cold, cold, bolted cellar.

Here candles, the recent options
Of romance or soft reserves,
Are my only light and warmth,
In a world where running water, medication,
Carols, are like dreams
Of stranded astronauts.

There was a time,
A thousand Krakatoas since,
When I despised the snow
Because of influenza
Or a bruise. Imagine!
Yet how can I laugh?
A different snow is falling now,
Each flake a murdering ghost
Of stranger, brother,
Sucked into service
Of an act once thought

Impossible; covering the city,
As I sit here squinting, shivering,
Waiting for death or worse,
Wondering where Christ is,
In this cold, cold, bolted cellar.

Ronald Parr

OUR FRIENDS LIE THERE

Our friends lie there beneath the
sweet green turf of Normandy. They
sleep, row on row as they have slept
for fifty years. We left them there
when we came home from war.

The children place their flowers
beside each small white stone. Innocent
tokens of their gratitude to soldiers
of the second war, who crossed the sea
to die for freedom's sake.

And we old men, veterans of that time
so long ago, when young men died to give
us lives of peace, return to pay our
homage, shed our tears, and hear their
voices in our dreams. They were our
friends, and we salute them, as they
        lie sleeping there.

Brian Gregan

TOO YOUNG TO DIE

How I remember my old mate, way back in forty-one.
We joined the ranks together, so young and full of fun.
We both had leave, the same weekend, to marry our loves true.
Before we joined the convoy, to sail the oceans blue.
After many weeks of sailing, we finally reached the foe.
We fought in heated jungle, our fate we did not know.
But Charlie didn't stand a chance, they shot him through the head
He lay there on the ground, so young, so cold, so dead.
His grave is overgrown now, forgotten, lost forever.
But for me, he still lives on, 'forgotten' never.

E K Wood

WHY HAVE WARS!

There's been World War One and World War Two
The War of the Roses so what's new?
The truth of the matter is it's still going on
In towns and cities great and small
With hatred, bitterness and anger increasing
There's no compromise and it's so frustrating,
Why can't love win over strife
Jesus used love to stop quarrels in folks' life,
If only mankind would love his neighbour.
Then no blood would be shed and life we could savour.
It's a terrible waste to take a life
And bereave a family or husband or wife.
Which is easier to love or hate?
It's up to us to decide our fate
Bombs destroy God's great creation.
His beautiful Earth and manifestation
Why have wars and bomb and bullet
When peace is better, so let's pursue it.
Encourage the leaders of countries and nations
To work towards peace and reconciliation.
One day man will get the message
And not make war a necessity or fettage.
Let the prayer for peace ring loud
And let us all the sound resound.
So God above will change men's hearts
And help us all not live apart,
But rather join in a united band
When nation and country will walk hand in hand.

Josephine Quinn

BLOOD HARVEST

No memorial
for the slaughtered

no obituary
for the victims

no comfort for
the raped

no rescue
for the helpless
hounded around
the barren land
to the place
of extermination

men
women
children
babies
hacked to death
in mindless
hatred

desperate
despairing children
lost and forsaken
seek everywhere
for dead parents

caring helpers
from another world
struggle to comfort
cure and feed

but

too few
too little
too late.

Stephen Gyles

SILENT NUMBERS

Silence sat upon the hill of death
No more words riding on man's breath
Emptiness filled the faces of the brave
As they lay numbered to take their grave

Some as old as youth, others in their prime
All dead before their time
War brought them to this place of grief
For death to steal them like a thief

Not one single tear can raise them from their sleep
For death is death and never was so deep
A piece of metal for a precious life
A pitiful token for their valiant strife

What is war for, but to maim and kill
To place an immortal soul without its will
Against a wall of strangers, just the same
These pawns, these men without a name

So to the victor let his glory be one of shame
For those numbers that died indeed in vain
And let those other pawns spared by death's ugly hand
Remember this had all been planned.

Cathrine Campbell Rogers

THE ATTACK

We were flying near the convoy, the vista quite serene,
Until the gunner shouted, 'I can see a submarine!'
She was floating on the surface about six miles away.
We're sure she hadn't seen us, as she stalked her heedless prey.

With the sun behind us we started out attack,
As diving on the target, we maintained a steady track.
Our Catalina Flying Boat had guns prepared and ready,
And all four lethal depth charges, now primed, 'neath wings,
                                                     held steady.

There were flashes from the guns below which meant we'd now
                                                     been seen,
But we pressed on quite regardless, as in a haunting dream.
Front guns were fired in rapid bursts at the 'deck crew' manning
                                                     the gun,
Then a crimson flash, and a sudden lurch, God - we've been hit
                                                     by the Hun!

Thick black smoke and acrid fumes filtered through from the
                                                   damaged bow,
With Captain hit and Gunner dead, what are our chances now?
No time to think, we're nearly there, our charges fall away,
Then the straddled hull just passed below, obscured beneath the spray.

The mist fell back into the sea, and left a picture clear,
As the tilted hull slid below the waves, we gave a doleful cheer.
What was the damage we'd sustained? We'll have to check and see!
Our 'Skipper' badly wounded and the aircraft could better be.

With radio messages cleared, we headed back to base,
Returning home to Sullom Voe, a bleak but friendly place.
How were we going to 'land' this hull which could clearly take
                                                     no more?
With decision quick, there was no choice, we'd beach it on the shore.

We alighted on the water and 'taxied' towards the land,
Then reduced speed very slowly to settle on the sand.
Help was very quick to come, with the doctor first on the scene,
What a wonderful sight to see, or was it just a dream?

Our mission was almost finished, with debriefing accompanied by tea,
It was just a routine Flying Boat trip, an epic of war at sea!

Reg Curwen

SWORDS AND SHARES

The words of power are beaten
into memory
Vows of fealty
long since have failed
Now it's just you
and me
for eternity.

The long ships have sailed
too far away
The old ways are
paved over
Will there be survivors
or victors
from the new war?

The winter hero
dies on an unknown shore
The summer monarch
is ignored:
An unseen flower
blooms in the desert night
What love provides
its sacred light?

Paul Thompson

WAR

A trembling heart so silent.
A thud that pierces the ear.
Trench of refuge, encountering the violent.
To foe, a brave, a tear and a prayer.

Blast shatters reluctant mist, bodies cold and still.
Screams echoed field of death.
A mother's tear, oh God, not our Bill.
Relief, her grateful breath.

So distant a land, valiant they fell.
Remember their souls, esteem dignity.
Oh Lord thine arms comfort, into thy kingdom dwell.
Our gratitude beyond compare, for now and eternity.

Oh Lord cast out evil and endless sorrow.
Make the world a fountain, love sprays upon.
And yesterday's wars, never tomorrow.
A coming dawn brings love, happiness, for everyone.

K Stackhouse

WAR CHILD

A child sat with tear stained face
    Bewildered and forlorn
War was always there from the day
    That they were born.

To eat each day no matter what
    A luxury they have not got
A quenching drink for longing thirst
    They'd walk for miles to get there first.

But little limbs were tired and weak
    Both old and young could hardly speak.
And yet we heard a baby cry
    The new arrive while others die.

Can this hell on earth be true.
    Aren't you glad it isn't you
Could we stand the heat, the flies.
    Hunger, thirst, war's built on lies.

Jennifer Statham

SOLDIERS

Empty trouser legs, for why?
Empty eye sockets, can't see the sky.
Unfeeling heart, numbed by war,
So what was it for? Too great the scar.

Nightmare nights full of fear,
Emptiness filled by shorts and beer,
Soaked in sweat voice ends in scream,
Oh to sleep and not to dream.

Empty place within the home,
Room prepared yet he still does not come.
See the photo, pride of place,
Memories sealed time can't erase.

Empty branch in family tree,
He gave his life so we could be free.
Tears run down the furrowed face
Thinking of lives war put to waste.

Judith E Lowe

No Surrender

Schools burning, churches ablaze
Homes destroyed, people afraid
Your day will never come
You are not wanted
Can you not hear
Out of our way, we're marching, keep clear
Fenian Bastards, Papal Scum

You will not pass
No Popish Mass
Will defile our town
We are the master race
Catholics remember your place
Taigs lie down

The streets are red
Policemen lie dead
For only doing their job
Keeping their patch clear
From mayhem and fear
Where are you hiding dear
God

Far away in London Town
Burning buildings come
tumbling down
Following a visit from the IRA
'No surrender' is the cry
No matter if folks hurt
or die
Victory will be ours one day

Most of us God
Both papist and Prod
Want this slaughter to cease
Our friendship's anew
Our faith in you too
Please God, please send us
peace

C Brady

KILLING TIME

If I move my shawl to there
So I am able
Not to see the other chair
Beside the table
If I watch the patterns on the cloth
Of shadow battles between lamp and moth
If I, unseeing, stare
If I do not move, nor speak, nor pray
I may find a way
Never to look into that space
Where, when the world made sense, I found your face
If I do not pause
To try to understand your cause
The things you said your duty made you do
Bloody, brutal things you said were good and true
If I no longer give
If, though I breathe, and feel, and weep
I do not live
May I not, too
Sink deep into that bitter sleep
And come to be with you?

Kathy Squires

PRISONERS OF TIME
(A prisoner-of-war camp in the Far East)

Concealed among the jungle trees
A prison camp lies derelict,
Where only whispers in the breeze
Pay tribute to a past conflict.

Abandoned barbed wire barriers rust
Around the long disused compound
To blend into the soft red dust
Where captives' blood once stained the ground.

On crumbling huts the monsoon rain
Beats wildly in a sudden surge.
It could not wash away the pain
Inflicted by the warder's scourge.

The rain beats down. I hear the sound
Of long dead voices through the trees.
The men whose spirits haunt this ground
Who died from hunger and disease.

Their ghostly forms in rank and file,
Once marched, impelled by dogged will
Or jested with defiant smile.
This place is haunted by them, still.

In sudden calm, the deluge ends
Steam rises from the forest floor.
And silence once again descends
On relics of a ruthless war.

A palm branch rustles through the air
To fall on ground where men once lay
Too weak to stand, as in despair
They thought of homes now far away.

Through all those years, they hoped each day
The war would end and set them free.
They did not know that they would stay
Imprisoned through eternity.

Nature has repossessed the land,
For now the forest trees have thrust
Through look-out posts no longer manned,
And dust once more returned to dust.

Mary Joyce Baxter

PEACE IS FINISHED

Sinn Fein have now admitted,
There is now no guarantee
That further IRA violence
Is not imminent to a degree.

We live with the vivid reality
Of an end to their cessation,
Republicans in Crossmaglen
Adding a chilling dimension.

They hoisted 'sniper at work'
On signposts around the village,
Showing a sniper with loaded gun,
Ready to deliver his carnage.

This sign is a red triangle,
In a corner is the legend
'I am back'. The sniper has killed
Eight soldiers in Northern Ireland.

Peace in Northern Ireland is now
Seen to be almost diminished,
We expect, and accept as fate,
That the peace process is finished.

Albert Wilson

Monsters

When I was a boy, one never forgets,
Blind young men, some with no legs,
Badly scarred, no hands, or arms,
I was a little frightened,
Yet they meant me no harm,
These, poor wretches, disfigured, and maimed,
Saliva, runs freely from those with no names,
Uncontrollable shaking, as if in a dance,
Yet others so stupid, as if in a trance,
Arms outstretched, feeling their way,
Unaided, they wander, out for the day,
Brain tissue scarred, they talk in a mumble,
People step to one side, when they fall and they tumble,
Bath chairs, and wheel chairs, a stroll in the park,
Some with pretty coloured ribbons,
Worn over their hearts,
Flat caps, and best suits, wet patches on pants,
Who are these monsters, that rave, and rants,
When I grew up, 'twas, then that I learned,
So much respect, from all, they had earned,
These monsters, were heroes, true as can be,
They were much better men, than you or me,
Afraid of the monsters, his young eyes saw,
In fact, they were, soldiers who fought in the war,
Many years have now passed, the boy is now old,
One thing he regrets, he wished he'd been told,
He'd seen so many people, injured, and maimed,
Perhaps, then, it was simply, so hard to explain . . .

J Smith

STRANGERS

Once again, May is here.
My thoughts stray back upon a tear
to forty-one, I can't forget
the hours we spent with strangers met
in some close of baffled walls.
Resounding round, the siren's call.

Was travelling home with a friend,
the tram stopped, we alighted. Then
shrapnel struck upon the ground.
Hurried on till shelter found
in a close with thirty folk.
Who laughed and sang, telling jokes

Inside me something! Had to leave!
My friend said, 'No!' But with my pleas
off we walked to digs we shared.
Left behind the strangers there,
Singing songs of yester-years.
Their voices ringing in our ears.

Next day, in the morning light,
the shelter shared that awful night.
Where thirty strangers joked and sang.
Never knew this day began!
For six and fifty years each May,
I spare a thought for them that day.

Jane Bhadal

A Soldier's Tale

I witnessed the ravaged lands of my birth
the grey scarred land with no growing worth
the trees were felled the water was sour
the green grass was dying hour by hour

Bombs rained down from above my head
a tear fell for my family dead
they were gone a long time ago
still the bombs rained down killing more

I tried and I fought to keep my land not alone
for there came thousands in hand
to fight for our freedom our homes and our people
they bombed our church with its ancient steeple.

Our homes were but rubble which littered the ground
a monument of sorts to what once stood around
the fountain no longer ran in town square
but we remembered what once had been there.

Barb wire fences search lights and planes
the sky burned red with buildings a flame
the sound of gun fire echoing fast another
life gone with every new blast. A woman
sobbed on bended knees death and grief were her
disease.

'I spoke to the Lord God himself before the battle
and asked this of him.'

'Flow fast Father Time I pray soon
all will be well we shall walk tall and strong
from these gates of hell into new
pastures of green and plenty
where our futures can grow happy and healthy
but for now we must face the fight in hand
we must try and save what's left of our land.
In God I trust and God I pray
Keep us safe another day.'

Gina Charles

DON'T WEEP FOR ME
(YUGOSLAVIA)

Don't weep for me, for I was only raped,
Friends, neighbours, hammered, then broke down the door,
Shouting, 'We have come for fun.'
Fun, with machete, knife and gun?
I was punched then kicked onto the floor,
Leering faces, groping hands, grunting, swearing,
Biting, slapping, clothing tearing.
My husband tried to fight,
Someone laughed and fired a bullet at his head,
My son, seven years old, so small and slight,
Not worth a bullet a machete would do for him
And like his father, he too, lay dead.
Then leaving me bruised and bleeding on the floor,
My friends, my neighbours, half ashamed, left,
No backward glance just kicking aside the broken door.
Don't weep for me, for I was only raped.

D W Owen

BAD MEMORIES

Never wanted it to happen,
        Didn't want it to start.
Now it's left many a soldier,
With an aching, breaking heart.
        War is worse than cancer
        Self-inflicted by man,
Many of you have forgotten
        I know I never can.
I'm an old man now
But I remember it clear,
        Young boys maimed and killed
Their poor faces etched with fear.
My best friend died
He lost both legs - dear Sam,
        He cried like a baby
And kept repeating mam - mam.
I came home in one piece
        He's lucky they said,
But I still suffer the nightmares
You'd not believe what goes on in my head.
        We must have peace
        Let this hell cease.

Beryl Spanswick

THEN AND NOW

It's fifty years or more now
Since our country went to fight
The 'tyrants' and oppressors,
We were sure that we were right.

When every night the bombs rained down
And people quaked with fright
The tracers flew and airmen knew
They'd die for what was right.

But still the nations quarrel
And do not heed the plight
Of the thousands who are suffering
To prove just who is right.

So when our chosen leaders
Wrestle late into the night
To see the other's points of view
We pray they will get things right.

Beatrice Jones

COMPASSION

It doesn't take much to start a war
An unkind word or even a brawl
Comradeship, seems to have gone,
Thoughts to help others
Compassion, long passed, all gone

People in war zones left dying
These are the scenes, that one sees
Battling soldiers, in those Killing Fields
Mud and disease catch up with the rest
All loved ones, no matter the creed,
Children and parents no respect for their need
Send in all the helpers this we do plead,

All that is done, is done with much care
But so much is needed give all you can spare
Such disgusting scenes, so unreal, we weep
Think to the future, our hearts sorely bleet.

Ruth Kirkham

BROTHERS

A boy of thirteen
Walks from school,
Whistling a tune,
Kicking a stone.
In occupied Poland.

Snatched by the Hun.
Imagine a mother,
Waiting in vain.
The anguish and pain
Where is he?

Three years labour
In a hellish camp.
His suffering obscene,
Still only sixteen,
The boy escapes.

Eating the roots
Raw, from fields.
Suckled by the cow,
God knows how.
But he survives.

The Polish army
Enlists the lad.
Fights in France,
Then, by chance,
He's in England.

Two old soldiers,
Polish and 'Tommy'
Re-live the war,
What they fought for.
Kids, grandchildren free.

Fifty years, friends.
Memories are dimming
Prompting each other,
As brother to brother
Sharing and caring.

The British soldier
Recalls Belsen Camp.
Same war, different story.

José Herron

WAR GAMES, 1914-1918

Proudly the soldiers marched along,
volunteers each, and every one,
Cheers from the crowds, that line the way,
how little did they know, that day,
For across the sea, in a part of France,
the German army, had orders to advance,
They bombarded the area, to be taken,
shells, and bullets fly, all hell awaken,
Bodies torn apart, men left to die,
from that ceaseless onslaught, from the sky,
There was no answer, or way to fight,
this fire power, of German might,
Twisted bodies, writhe in pain,
as they clawed at the mud, in the driving rain,
Men lay where they fell, some never to be found,
as the endless salvo, raked the ground,
Those at home, could never imagine, or see,
the death, and destruction, that was to be,
For those volunteers, and enlisted men,
many never seen, again,
They were called to arms, by the powers to be,
while they sat in their office, and sipped their tea.

Colin Dudley

SEA OF POPPIES

Poppies sway gently in the breeze
Over the many fields.
Once many bodies lay
In those peaceful fields.

From Norman times to present day
Those fields have felt.
The pain and anguish of
Many a man.

Eventually those many voices
Were heard.
And those fields remain
Still over Normandy.

But what of those other
Killing fields.
When will God hear those
Have we got to wait
For millions of more men
To die.
Before those fields sway
With poppies once more.

D Selbie

SABOTAGE

Light the fuse and go to ground.
Press the plunger. Hear the sound
As the bridge goes up, and the train
Rolls down, in mute material pain.

One man can do this with the knack,
And right equipment in his pack.
One man who hates the endless drill,
And of mute obedience had his fill.

In Roman times he had no scope,
To wet this mood of misanthrope.
But now the plant is built the target large,
Fit bull's eye for his sabotage.

From Lawrence to Wingate to SOE
Men have followed their own corps d'esprit.
So bearing in mind the above mentioned circs,
Shouldn't we call it: 'a spanner in t'works'?

James Stevenson

TEARS ROLL DOWN

Beside the baked earth road they lay
Their tiny outstretched hands that beg for help
But no-one looks their way.
Numbed by war their silent tears run cold
Forgotten innocence and love once more,
Shattering their souls.
Through haunted eyes the starving children see
Longing for the peace of death that freedom brings -
For all eternity.
In silent darkness we always hide our eyes
From children used as shields of innocence
In a war of genocide
And we pray to God for his forgiveness
For the atrocities of our time
And hope one day we will remember
The innocence of a child.

Greg King

IN THIS AGE

In this age of great despair
Thoughts are needed and deep prayer
Once in death remorse was felt
There's a corpse but no pelt

Poverty seems on the increase
Futuristic ideas for peace
Council tenants all appalled
Rent collectors withered and bald

Drink and drugs seem the answer
Heavy debts seem to incur
For a high of seconds only
No money left for alimony

Turn to the press what do you see
Suicides were they related to you or me
Why do they do it? What goes wrong!
Perhaps they listened to the wrong song

Is that a light we see will politics change
No it's the guns firing on the range
Off to battle the Sappers go
Are they frightened . . . Oh no . . .

Iraqi missiles soar sky high
What's it for? Prayers are nigh
IRA are on the attack
Kids on the street are taking smack

Advice is high and morale's low
The human race has far to go
One thing in common rings true
What are we here for what's our due

Ann Hubbard

ARMAGEDDON

The pestilence of war, forever trundling on,
Oh, sound the death - knell again and again
For what does it matter when living things die?
'Some will survive - and some will perish',
Has always been mankind's bitter cry!

The pointing, accusatory finger, young men,
Your mothers bore you all, for this, it decrees,
To take up your arms and defend what is right
And to lay down your lives, with God on your side,
You surely must see, thro' the darkness, the light?

Turn away from the suffering, deprivation and shame,
On *your* shoulders there can be no blame!
You only obey what your leaders decree -
Young men, take up arms and just follow me!
We'll blast them and burn them,
Until 'Mercy' they scream,
And bomb them and rape them
And pillage their dream!

From cradle to grave, just do as you're told,
To question superiors - do *not* be so bold!
For metal was surely devised for killing -
Fall in, young men, and show you are willing
To maim and to torture
Fellow creatures like you,
Just because they are 'different' -
Yes, Christ was a Jew!

'Love thy neighbour as thyself'
And war will recede,
But 'Armageddon' may come
Ere the learning is done.

Julia Eva Yeardye

WHAT IT WOULD BE LIKE

Why can't there be peace in this world, just for a day.
Just imagine what it would be like,
If all religions, all races, become friends.
The thing is all we will be able to do is, imagine this.
It's never going to happen
The generation before me thought the same thing,
and no doubt, the next generation will also think the same way.
Is there any sense in even dreaming about peace,
There's certainly no sense in talking about it,
There's too much hate in this world,
Too many evil people.
I suppose the best thing I can do,
is make sure I am never at fault myself
But I am just one in many,
A needle in a haystack
Please, look inside your very souls
And there if you look hard enough, you will find peace
Do this for the sake of the next generation
And please do it now.

Steven Hunter

VIEW FROM DEATH HILL

Once lush with corn and
seasonal crop
God's creatures lie low:
the hunters and the hunted
in the fields below -

Soldiers, civilians,
animals, reptiles, birds,
butterflies, insects and
flowers.

Now Death Hill looks
down on desolation, while
the dead abide their time.

Remember the flowers:
marigolds, poppies, purple
creepers demanding space -
mown down not by gunshot
or machete

but by chemicals?

Arda Lacey

THE UNINVITED GUEST

We sit by an empty chair
Listening to people not there.
Hearing stories they can not tell,
Of soldiers, and heroes, who fell,
At the Somme or Alamein.
Of wars made by the insane
As we sit and stare
At the futile mocking empty chair.
Stories come of showers and stars;
Of people loaded in railway cars.
Travelling to their doom
Through death smoke gloom.
Men in black made of stone
Following orders, forgetting to atone.
Stories come from the chair
From people forever there
Listening to all and learning none
We still have war, have the gun.

Teresa Whaley

Forgiven

My heart within your sights
You aim along the barrel
And think not of consequences
Of widows in black
And bitter children
They know not, how I wish they could
Feel the pity I feel for you
A life, a death, a moment in time
Hot lead shoots true yet
You cannot see it strike
You cannot feel its pain
Your act is born not of hatred
But of high command from
A face you've never seen
A man you've never met
Yet he is someone you will kill for, will die for
Am I your enemy or your brother in chaos?
You fight for the right cause, but so do I
Are we so different?
No I think we are alike
Had I got you in my sights
I too would have fired
I see you not as a man but
As an order, something I'm obliged to do
A pain I cannot feel
A threat I have ended
I understand
But your aim was true
Can you feel justified?
Just know that you are forgiven.

Phil Simpson

What Price A Life?

The staring eyes
The soulless cries
A sudden shriek
Another dies

A babe alone
A blanket torn
No-one to weep
No-one to mourn

The naked fear
The evil leer
A fateful blow
A silent tear

The blood has run
The deed is done
No-one can gain
No-one has won

The price is high
The bodies lie
Grotesquely strewn
Waiting to die

How can it be
Can no-one see
The utter waste
The futility.

S Griffiths

DEAD SOLDIER REINCARNATION

A mere ghost of the past now,
I look up, recalling various ends,
numerous last skies merging
upon my heart's many last beats.

Plunged, bayoneted, skewn,
my lungs punched through -
I remember Flanders and
the poppies and the breeze that blew,

my eyes gouged out with spoons,
I fought in Jacobean skirmishes
and slipped a dagger under
rare, rich ribs in plunder of jewels,

and my feet hacked off squarely
with saw blades, by those scoundrels
searching about for old boots
and gold caps in the inferno,

my lungs removed by nerve gas
when the mask slipped out
of my grip; snatched in
the hot selfishness of preservation.

And now,
from my dilapidated corpus,
I see a new cloud approaching,
racing over the horizon,

rallying over divisions
of newer, more terrible tanks,
more lethal, invisible forces
'neath whose war-tuned wheels I'll fall.

David Miller

THE THEATRE OF WAR

Curtain up on the theatre of war.
Starring; in an all male cast;
Man, and his kind. Running now to
Packed houses for six thousand years, always
The same theme, blood, rich red blood,
The cream of the nation. Nothing has
Changed, only the methods of murder, mayhem
And butchery. Silly man and his kind
Always at the ready; but never for
A loaf of bread, better homes or a
Better life.

Who to study in this homicidal play,
With its all male cast; the women folk
Are left behind to mind the kids.
Hecuba must weep for women and orphaned
Children. Andromache must weep for soldier husband.
Priam must go-a-begging for bodies of
Dead sons, packed in body bags, and pay
The asking price, and kiss all cheeks
For the favour. Greeks must from the foul
Womb of the wooden horse and become pyromaniacs
And child killers. Man, must study the
Man in all mankind, for in each man's
Breast is the soul of Cadmus; who sowed
The dragon's teeth; in this homicidal theme,
Upon which the curtain never comes down,
Is a popularity in perpetuity.

G Kenny

LORD HAVOC!

Blood drips heavy, like honey upon the green-suede,
Falling blindly from the freshly decorated blade,
A body stark and full of hate,
Sends another companion to the traitor's fate.
The battle's roar is long since gone,
And a deathly silence lingers on,
A demon soul cries out this night,
To challenge all within its sight,
The headless horseman rides again,
Across the land of Charlemagne,
Valiant fellows fall down dead,
When they see the horseman's head,
Skewered upon his ancient lance,
It leads his foes a merry dance,
For every man who see'd his eyes,
Was struck by fear and terrorised,
Hold fast! Cruel heart! You'd hear them bawl,
Then you'd hear the horseman call,
Cry havoc! And ring that ghostly bell!
We ride this night through the Gates of Hell!

C N Messenger

THE DARKEST MOMENTS

In the darkest moments
When frustration helps the mind
To wander
I contemplate
On one's idealism
On one's aim in life
On one's struggle
To find fulfilment
On one's hardship
For the want
Of a better life

In the darkest moments
When depression dissolves
An active mind
I hesitate
On one's role in life
On one's goal in life
On one's life
And in how one walks it
Is the track to the left or right?
One never knows
The answer is always hidden
Around the corner

Kevin Murphy

LIVING TO FIGHT

Fighting to live - living to fight
Who's to say if the world's wrong or right.
A means to an end, is the cause worth the cost
Does anybody count the lives that are lost.
Dinner conversation, a topic of news
As we sit around the table airing our views.
Judging the motives, pouring pity and scorn
Commenting on the orphaned and forlorn.

Don't waste your tears on the dead, they are gone
Feel pity and sorrow for those who live on.
Maimed and in pain, lost a limb not a life
Families torn apart, lost both child and wife.
Home is but rubble, the future's not bright
Does anybody really understand their plight.
How deep is the caring, will anybody give
The comforts of life to help others live.

Zenda Cooper

STOP, YOU'RE KILLING ME!

They say that when your name is on the bullet
Your time is up. (Kill one.)
But how many names can you inscribe on a magazine clip?
(Kill a dozen.)
More, perhaps, on a bomb casing. (Kill thousands.)
Lots more on the red button that triggers The Bomb.
(Kill millions.)
OK let's go for Global Nuclear Warfare.
(Kill the lot.)
Who wins then? No survivors. No-one left. Nobody.
Pathetic, isn't it? Literally fatalistic isn't it?
So why do we do it?

T Pemberton

BRAVE SOLDIER

I know a soldier
Who is far away . . .
He lies in the sand
And waits for his prey . . .

He cleans his weapon
So shiny and bright
This bit of metal that catches the light . . .
Don't cry for this soldier
Who's out in the Gulf . . .
He's there for us all
As he tries to stop the wolf . . .

This man is the leader of Iraq
No borders can save him
From this soldier's attack . . .

Go good soldier
To battle they say . . .
Don't be long good soldier
We want you home one day . . .

Peter Frost

PRISONERS OF WAR

You get a horrible feeling when you're
Trapped
As though you've lost your mind.
You see the pain and suffering
Of people your own kind.
Trapped in a hard dark cell,
Where from it comes sad moans and yells.
Infected with some parasite
Which attacks morning, noon and night
Inflicted with endless pain
I wish they'd realise it isn't a game
Shattered bodies, shattered minds,
Always murderous, never kind,
Lots of tears have to be shed,
Before anything can be said.
Lots of luck has to come,
Before anything can be done.
Please don't plot against us,
Please contribute towards us.
We are the prisoners of war.

Lauren Sirey

War Again

They build their ships
ready for warfare
again and again
famous war men
owning land, living grandé
other men are sent insane from
explosions, hand-grenades and bombs
the noises never fade for them
may be they regret
What is fair in war
again and again
in wars there's so much stress
and also such distress
war only causes pain
again and again
people suffering children maimed
made homeless, made parentless or even killed
again and again
They're sent to empty orphanages
who cares anyway, they owe a debt
the only way, some will say
to make them pay, their debts
to war, again and again
It's a mean game to ransom people
with expensive planes for debts
again and again
The veterans they survive
The babies they do not
They are just forgot.

J Dunkley

Bert 1641095

The bandsmen were playing down on the quay
In farewell to the lads being shipped o'er the sea
Smartly uniformed in airforce blue, these young men
Were off to fight in a foreign land, ravaged by war and mayhem.
On board they were given their orders, this ground based crew
Aircraft recovery was what they were assigned to do.
Dive bombed and shelled the ship docked in a bay
The pier, tangled and smashed had been blown far away.
No-one warned them of the ear-splitting noise, and
The foul smell of death from bodies strewn on the sand.
They dodged and scrambled as they raced from the waters
Praying to be out of this chaos and into their quarters.
For three long years the lads did their duties
Tending aircraft that were hit and crashed down into pieces.
They dragged from the wreckage pilots without faces, body
                                              charred black.
His buddies blasted into shreds were swept up into a sack,
Hearts and emotions were on hold, and eyes tried not to see
The horror of all this carnage, that went on endlessly
Parts that could be salved from the mangled charade
Were placed in a pile, called the aircrafts' graveyard.
May it rest in peace with the men and pilots who flew them
For those that survived, live haunted by the death of those proud men.
Death is the victor, we know that from the time we are born
War destroys, it cripples and maims, left are widows and mothers
                                              who mourn,
Why cannot men except life is a gift of ten and three score
And fill it with happiness, and say, no more, no more, to war.

E Merritt

REMEMBRANCE

No grave that rests in distant foreign earth,
Could hide the spirit of their freedom cries.
Who sallied forth, far from their land of birth,
And in the final loneliness of conflict dies.

Poppies red, a mantle for the myriad that fell,
Among the blood-soaked trenches of a Flanders' field.
While gratitude for sacrifice, the poppy wearers tell,
And older hearts, their sadness, in quietness concealed.

Thirty-nine, another time, horror of war enslaves,
With armies fighting through the years in places far.
Merchant sailors, dangers face upon the ocean's waves
Brothers in arms with naval friends, the bold jack-tar.

Civilians caught up in the fray, reveal their spirit too,
At home, and with the ARP they pay a heavy price.
The conflict in the sky, the glorious 'few'.
And others serving in the air, prepared for sacrifice.

Since then, gaps, among the fragile years of peace,
The Falklands, Desert Storm, their victims claim.
So praying that we learn, and wars may cease.
For; if we remember not, 'They died in vain'.

Dennis Brockelbank

OUR GARDEN IN WINTER

Weary, weary Northern Ireland dreary;
How does your garden grow?
Through this long bleak wintertime
Of nigh thirty years we know?
Where are all the flowers gone,
That once we hoped to see?
Gone! I fear, beyond recall
To this benighted country.
Where are all the gardeners gone
Whose words helped us to dream?
Gone! I fear, beyond recall;
Banished by that last scream.
Where are all the seeds they had
To make our garden grow?
Gone! I fear, beyond recall
To the sad land of Limbo.
What of all the promises
They never did fulfill?
Buried, I fear, beyond recall
In that cemetery on the hill.
Where are the men who made them
In those days long gone?
Gone! I fear, beyond recall;
Leaving our futures all in pawn.
What shall we do now, then;
With the Final Darkness closing in?
Can we not speak to each other?
Let some new light and ideas in?
'Tis only by such talking
That any war can end.
'Tis only by reaching agreement
We can call each other 'friend'.
'Tis only by building friendships
That true peace comes, in the end.

J Nolan

WHERE LIES

Men up to their knees in mud, cold, broken, disorientated
Eyes empty of all emotion, their thoughts triggered only
from orders,
Their lamented songs no longer,

A bloody whistle blow and everyone goes over,
Boys and men the same, all slaughtered,
Lost in smoke shaken by shell,
Trapped in fire from the endless bullet hail,
As the last flare goes down we lie fumbling in our minds,
For our bodies lie stiff as lead close to the grave,
And there we wait, until the guns sleep,
Only the chattered burst of machine gun fire reach
Out to those demented cries their sound as laughter
In fits of rage beyond the fall to cratered graves.

Bodies strewn across stretchers come back to haunt
Us, torn relics of men and boys once like us
Now more like those beyond us,
Some wave some cry or prolong their last agonising
Breath for life,
Death becomes us,

Peace passes over like a moment of thought in this gutter,
And in a moment of thought hell swallows up
          The forgotten soldier.

Mark Andrew Phillips

SUMMER OF 1940

As I remember
it was a hot summer's day
    and the battle for the skies
over Britain was now in full swing
    I was stationed at Biggin Hill
with the RAF
    as a fighter pilot with three kills to my name
three, four sorties a day
    trying to stop the Hun from controlling our skies
many of my friends were killed
    during that bloody summer
in my spare time I used to lounge around
    sometimes a game of cricket
or a doze in the sun
    then a cry of 'scramble'
as we hurried to get the Spits into the sky
    but today I remember with sadness
it was the day that my brother died
    I just couldn't help him
for I was in a dogfight
    being shot to pieces by a 109
I tried to outsmart him
    banking to the left
then to the right
    within seconds my Spit was on fire
and I had to get out
    for I was one of the lucky ones
who got out alive
    but for my brother
his Spit exploded in the sky

Anthony Clarke

BATTLE CRY

We rose at dawn, mad screaming
to fields of crimson fire,
dusk found us lay undreaming,
amongst the shattered wire.

The tearing sound of incoming rounds,
a gut felt numbing thud,
then a flower of brown earth blossoms
where comrades had been stood.

A sudden sense of inner peace.
I watch detached, as in a dream,
A dark pool wetly spreading
where once a leg had been.

There's a coldness like I've never known
then pain's reality comes.
Soon a shrill and constant screaming
rises high above the guns.

Now pain ebbs slowly sweet away
pulse an ever fading drum,
Oh Jesus No! Not here. Alone.
Why doesn't someone come?

P K Church

THE HOLOCAUST

In parts of the world, people queue for miles,
their faces are sad with not any smiles.
Now times are hard without any bread,
as the hungry children cry to be fed.

But how do you feed an army so vast,
when corn never grew as it did in the past.
There's no nourishment in the ground any more,
which is all due to a nuclear war.

Of course those brave people deep underground,
locked in their bunkers, all safe and sound.
With plenty of food to last them for years,
while waiting in safety till the harmful ray clears.

There deep in shelters they dine with wine,
where the air is filtered, and everything's fine.
They listen to sounds which come from up top,
from agonised people, who are screaming none-stop.

If only they had stopped the rockets they hurled,
instead of pressing a button destroying their world.
Now they have sentenced themselves to a tomb underground,
where they sit waiting to start the next round,

Now these horrific dreams I would like to share,
while twisting and turning in my nightmare.
With a sweating brow I awake from my sleep,
and I lay in my bed now a quivering heap.

But I thank God it was only a dream,
but it seemed so real, if you know what I mean.
So I ask all those who argue the toss,
remember the man who carried the cross.

J W Hayes

SOMEONE TO BLAME

I danced with shadows through the night,
And sprouted wings and then took flight,
Way up above to smoke filled clouds,
Away from all the harmful crowds.

Then I descended from up high,
Back down into the battle's eye,
Taking care of other's notions,
While drowning in my emotions.

I fought so hard for kings and queens,
Who promised things beyond my dreams,
They said the world's for the taking,
But my body won't stop shaking.

The reality from within,
Is why hide behind anything,
For any moment I could die,
Without knowing the reasons why.

Forget all those who've promised all,
They're only friends until I fall,
Then no-one wants to know my name,
Except when there's someone to blame.

Philip Q Mills

AT WAR!

For a hundred years and more,
Countries have gone to war.
What is it all about?
Can anyone figure it out.

> A piece of land,
> A beach of sand,
> A craggy hill,
> For this; people kill!

When will this killing cease;
Has man become worse than the beasts?
When will people pause, and count the cost,
Or perhaps man's sanity is already lost.

B M Lennox

THE SILENCE

The silence of the crowded forest
The sheen of innocent pale white eyes,
       exposing nothing of the age of bloodshed
Laying stagnant, sheltered by the once
       blood-soaked foliage
The extensive dim of an escaping twig
       arousing the forest out of its fallacious peace
The lone bead of sweat running past his pale white eyes
Another warrior numb to the pain
The silence of the crowded forest, remains.

Clarissa Fear

THE WAUGH AGAINST CRIME

Let us remember how Auberon once,
Looked down a barrel to find some response.
The damned thing had jammed and he wondered for why,
So he leapt from his Scout Car and applied his right eye.
There was nothing to see but a barrel so clean
That he gave it a shake to wake up the dead stream.
The sleepers awoke and with chattering spite,
Made a hole in his shoulder, to let in the light.
Now Auberon the warlike, the expert in arms,
Wants to licence the public to shoot when alarmed.
But first let us teach them rule Catch 22,
If it's not properly applied it will blow you up too.

James Stevenson

INFORMATION

We hope you have enjoyed reading this book - and that you will continue to enjoy it in the coming years.

If you like reading and writing poetry drop us a line, or give us a call, and we'll send you a free information pack.

Write to :-
**Poetry Now Information
1-2 Wainman Road
Woodston
Peterborough
PE2 7BU
(01733) 230746**